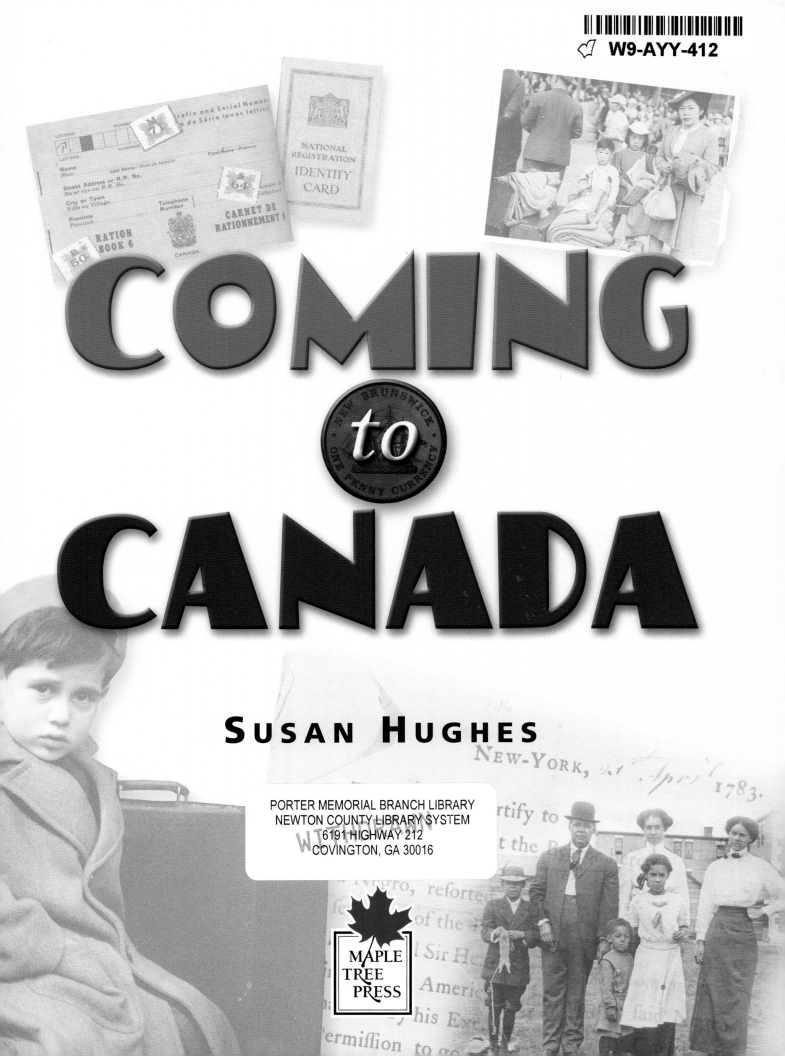

COMING *to* CANADA

SUSAN HUGHES

MAPLE TREE PRESS

Maple Tree Press Inc.

51 Front Street East, Suite 200, Toronto, Ontario M5E 1B3

www.mapletreepress.com

Distributed in Canada by Raincoast Books

9050 Shaughnessy Street, Vancouver, British Columbia V6P 6E5

Distributed in the United States by Publishers Group West

1700 Fourth Street, Berkeley, California 94710

Cataloguing in Publication Data

Hughes, Susan, 1960–

      Coming to Canada: building a life in a new land / Susan Hughes.

(A Wow Canada! book)

Includes index.

ISBN 1-897066-45-7 (bound).–ISBN 1-897066-46-5 (pbk.)

1. Canada–Emigration and immigration–History–Juvenile literature.

2. Canada–Population–Ethnic groups–History–Juvenile literature.

I. Title. II. Series: Wow Canada! book.

FC608.I4H83 2005   j971.004   C2005-901170-X

Design: Word and Image Design Studio

Image credits: See page 110

We acknowledge the financial support of the Canada Council for the Arts, the Ontario Arts Council, the Government of Canada through the Book Publishing Industry Development Program (BPIDP), and the Government of Ontario through the Ontario Media Development Corporation's Book Initiative for our publishing activities.

Printed in Hong Kong

A   B   C   D   E   F

CONTENTS

GOING WEST

A NEW CENTURY

The Changing Face of Canada

The Quilt of Belonging

Did you know that there is someone from every single country in the world living in Canada? Esther Bryan will tell you that. She's an artist who has become an expert on all the different people who make up this nation. Born in France to an American mother and a Slovakian father, she came to Canada with her family when she was only ten. When she was in her twenties, and just starting out as an artist, her father asked her to go to Slovakia with him for a visit.

That journey convinced Esther to explore her experiences as an immigrant returning home. She created artwork reflecting her visit and displayed the pieces in an exhibition called "Return." Before she knew it, others were sharing their own stories of immigration with her. "People had a hunger to have their stories told," Esther recounts. "They were saying, 'Include me. You don't know what I've gone through.'"

She soon came up with a brilliant idea: she decided to make a quilt about coming to Canada. Each piece, or block, of the quilt would represent a different ethnic or cultural group and be made by a person from the country or territory it stood for.

This block from Papua New Guinea is made from traditional *tapa* cloth, which comes from the bark of a mulberry tree. Instead of selling off the timber from their fragile rainforest, Papua New Guineans harvest the bark for *tapa* cloth from the mulberry trees flourishing in their own gardens.

Villagers in the Central African Republic gather delicate butterfly wings from the rainforest floor and use them for many artistic purposes. In this block, they create a typical village scene of women performing a ritual task.

Realizing a Dream

Right away, the idea took hold. People across Canada began submitting blocks, thrilled to share their cultural history through fabric and design. In what seemed like no time, several blocks were done. But tracking down at least one Canadian representative from each country in the world wasn't easy. In some cases, it took thousands of phone calls and letters, as well as help from the United Nations and the Canadian government, to find people to work on specific blocks. In the end, more than a thousand staff and volunteers worked for about five years to create the quilt.

The finished project is more than thirty-five metres long and three metres tall, and it has 263 blocks. "Each First Nations, Metis, and Inuit group in Canada is represented by its own block on the first row, which is the foundation row, and up the two sides," says Esther. "They wrap the quilt, which shows respect for these founding nations." Then there are 194 other blocks, one for each country in the world. "Each block has its own separate space, and yet is connected to the next block with a continuous length of cording," she explains. It symbolizes the separate but united cultures that make up Canada. "The quilt," she says, "shows our vision of the way we should live as a global family and as a Canadian family, [in a country] where there is a place for every individual."

The Guatemala block shows the country's national bird, the Quetzal, looking down on some stylized people, animals, trees, and a typical Guatemalan home. In the borders outside the centre square sit traditional "worry dolls." Many Guatemalans believe that any problems they tell to their worry dolls at night will have disappeared when the sun rises the next morning.

The First Immigrants to Canada

T his is a book about Canadians. And that means this book is actually about immigrants, because Canada is made of people who've come here from every country in the world. Fired with determination and courage, steeled with resolve, these people made their way here across land and sea to start a new life. They brought with them the words, skills, and memories of what had been, and they worked to create a new vision of what could be. The sons and daughters, and grandsons and granddaughters, of those immigrants have lived long on this land, slowly and steadily transforming the visions of their ancestors into new traditions and weaving them into their own lives. These many hands have created the spectacular quilt that is Canada.

This is a book about Canadians. It will tell some of the stories of those who have immigrated here, but nowhere near all of them. The threads in the quilt are just too many for that. But if you keep your eyes and ears open, listening to the stories of those around you, you'll find that many more fascinating tales will come your way. Every Canadian has an important story to tell of how someone in the family came to be here. Some came to Canada only yesterday and others came before the country even had a name, so the stories are never-ending and some reach back a long, long time.

This broken lance point, found on an island in the St. Lawrence River, is about 8,000 years old. It is evidence of the existence of some of the very earliest Canadians.

Coming to Canada

Exactly how long have people been coming to Canada? Two hundred years? Three hundred? Try 12,000 to 30,000 years! No one is certain of precisely when or how they came, but many scientists believe that the first people to reach Canada crossed here over a land "bridge" that once linked Siberia to what is now Alaska. If you look at your atlas, you can see where the bridge would have been, running across the Bering Strait to the northwestern corner of North America. It would have formed sometime between 75,000 and 14,000 years ago, as the last ice age was ending. Areas once covered with glaciers grew bare, and land once loaded down with ice lifted in relief.

So who were those first immigrants to Canada? Well, they might have been Stone Age hunters chasing animal herds as they migrated in search of food. Some geologists believe that gaps in the massive ice sheets covering prehistoric Canada created ice-free corridors that these early people could have followed south into the heart of the continent. Others think they might have been able to make their way down the western coast at a time when it was not covered in ice.

The First Peoples have been fishing Canada's waters and hunting its coastlines for at least 12,000 years.

These petroglyphs, found near Nanaimo, British Columbia, are perhaps a thousand years old. They show mythological sea creatures, wolves, fish, and even humans, and they have survived all this time despite the damage brought by nature and the curiosity of modern humans.

But other scientists disagree with these theories. They don't believe that water levels ever dropped far enough to expose a land bridge, and they insist that the freezing climate would never have permitted people to survive long enough to make their way across it. Their own theory is that the first people came to the western hemisphere *before* there was an open passage through the ice sheet. How? Perhaps by boat from Asia, Australia, or Siberia. Some anthropologists believe that humans were capable of ocean journeys as long as 30,000 years ago. They point out that the sea current that runs between Japan and the western coast of North America could have made a journey across the Pacific Ocean possible.

However they got here, those first arrivals were the ancestors of Canada's Native peoples—and the first immigrants to Canada. Others came after them, by foot or by boat. And as time passed, they came by horse and by train.

This ceramic pot dates from a period of Native culture sometimes called the Old Woman Phase. It was found in southern Manitoba in the early 1900s and is probably about 1,300 years old.

They arrived on sailing ships, on steamships, and on ocean liners. More recently, they have travelled by airplane, reducing the once exhausting trip from months, weeks, and days to a matter of hours. The tremendous journeys of the early migrants to this land have been repeated over and over again by others. But no matter how they got here, all those who have come have sought the same things as those first immigrants to Canada—safety, resources, a better and more prosperous life. They've shared something else as well—a spirit of adventure.

No one is really sure where the first people to come to Canada journeyed from. But we do know that people all over the world have been on the move for a very long time. There is evidence of our earliest ancestors making their way from Africa to the Middle East as much as 100,000 years ago. About 50,000 years ago, they began to spread east, to Southeast Asia, and west, to Europe. They travelled by boat to Australia around 35,000 years ago, and by 8000 B.C., 10,000 years ago, they had occupied just about the entire modern world. In fact, only a few islands, such as the Azores and the Seychelles, and some extreme environments, like the Arctic and Antarctica, remained uninhabited until more modern times.

Top: Found at a site in Labrador, this ivory mask dates from about 1 A.D. The Dorset peoples who would have carved this mask were descended from the original inhabitants of Canada's Arctic. *Bottom*: This strange-looking tool, which also dates from about 1 A.D., is a bark shredder. These were used, mostly by women, to peel the bark off trees. The bark was then pounded flat and treated with fish oil to make it water-resistant. It would be made into everything from pots to rain capes.

Building a Nation

Nous Sommes Ici

There were a few visitors to the coasts of this vast continent after the First Peoples made North America their new home, but it would be thousands of years before anyone else tried to settle permanently in Canada. Those who did come—the Norse around 1000 A.D., Portuguese and Basque fishermen in the 1500s—stayed for only short periods of time, then returned quickly to more welcoming lands.

But that all changed in 1604, when a French merchant named Pierre Du Gua de Monts gathered together about eighty brave adventurers and struck out across the ocean to establish a new colony on the east coast of North America, in the land that came to be called Acadia.

Unfortunately, de Monts and his colonists suffered horribly during their first year in Acadia, on an island in what is now Maine. The winter was harsh and bitter, disease attacked the settlers, and more than half perished before the spring came. As soon as they could, the starving, exhausted survivors relocated to a place they called Port-Royal, on the northwestern shore of Nova Scotia.

At Port-Royal, the Acadians put up solid buildings and even made dykes to hold back the ocean tides and create rich, fertile farmland.

There, with the help of the local Mi'kmaq, they learned how to survive in their challenging new home. They stocked up on food for the endless winter days that lay ahead and traded iron tools for fresh meat and warm furs.

The First Acadians

Port-Royal quickly became a thriving settlement, thanks mostly to this trade in furs with the Mi'kmaq. Europeans needed an almost constant supply of beaver pelts for the fur hats that had become so fashionable in cities like London and Paris. That made the fur posts in the North American colonies extremely valuable to their European owners.

Because Port-Royal was such a successful fur post for the French, it was soon also being claimed by England. In fact, in 1613 British settlers from Virginia raided the settlement and ran off the French colonists. A few years later, in 1621, the English government renamed all of Acadia New Scotland, or Nova Scotia, and moved in Scottish settlers to strengthen its claim to the land.

The French settlement at Louisbourg, on Cape Breton Island, thrived because it was right on the trade routes and its waters were full of valuable cod. At its height, about 4,000 people lived within the walls of the fortress.

But the French weren't going to give up their territory that easily. In 1632, a few hundred "gentlemen of quality" journeyed across the ocean to re-establish the French presence in Acadia. They built outposts all along the coast of Nova Scotia and what is now New Brunswick, and they fought the English for control of the fur trade.

For the next several decades, the land passed back and forth between the two powers, until it was delivered into the hands of the English one final time in 1713. To protect what little was left of their interests in Atlantic Canada, the French built a massive fortress, called Louisbourg, at Cape Breton Island. Then the two warring nations settled into an uneasy truce, with the British making no real effort to colonize their territory and the French enjoying the prosperity of the cod fishery in and around Louisbourg.

But in the 1750s, the British began to take a closer look at what they had in Nova Scotia. They moved the capital from Port-Royal to the better-situated Halifax and brought in thousands of new settlers. They then tried to force the French-speaking Acadians to swear an oath of loyalty to the Crown. Although the Acadian people had long ceased thinking of themselves as French, they had no particular allegiance to Britain either. When they refused to take the oath, the British saw an opportunity to end their dispute with France once and for all. They decided to round up all the Acadians and drive them from their homes.

Many Acadians were called to their parish church to hear the order of expulsion read out by British soldiers.

The Grand Dérangement

This Grand Dérangement, or Great Expulsion, was a time of sorrow and fear for the Acadian people. Shiploads of soldiers arrived and made prisoners of all they met. Some Acadians escaped into the woods, but many more were forced aboard the ships while their homes were burned behind them. Separated from friends and family, these fourth- and fifth-generation Canadians were sent to faraway American colonies they'd never seen before, like Georgia and Louisiana, and even to France or England.

Incredibly, many of the expelled Acadians did manage to make their way home again. After 1763, when hostilities between England and France eased once more, they were given permission to return, although not to their own lands, which had mostly been taken over by British settlers. Instead, they started all over again, settling mainly uninhabited coastal areas, such as the north shore of New Brunswick, the southwest coast of Nova Scotia, and the island of Cape Breton.

By the time of Confederation, in 1867, there were 87,000 Acadians living in Canada; today there are nearly half a million. These Canadians work hard to keep alive their unique, centuries-old heritage. They have their own national anthem, and the Acadian flag flies proudly from many Maritime rooftops. In 2004, Nova Scotia even hosted a celebration to mark the 400th anniversary of the founding of Acadia. Hundreds of thousands of people from France, Louisiana, and the rest of Canada came to meet their fellow Acadians and celebrate their common ancestry.

Evangeline Bellefontaine was the fictional Acadian heroine of a famous poem by Henry Wadsworth Longfellow.

The stained-glass windows of the chapel in Grand Pré, Nova Scotia, tell the tragic story of the Great Expulsion to all who visit.

The Filles du Roi

In 1608, Samuel de Champlain supervised the building of his Habitation at Quebec, proudly raising the flag of France when it was done. This modest fort was his only real home for the rest of his life.

Samuel de Champlain, the young mapmaker on Pierre de Monts's first settlement attempts in Acadia, eventually struck off on his own and led a group of colonists down the St. Lawrence River to Quebec. At the foot of a massive cliff, he began building a Habitation that he believed would be the foundation for a permanent, prosperous settlement.

Working hard to fulfil his dream, Champlain crossed the ocean twenty times to promote Quebec to potential colonists. Slowly, the settlement began to grow. Soon it had a church, some warehouses, and several homes, in addition to the buildings of the original Habitation. New colonists crossed the sea to make a life in Quebec, and many brought their families with them.

But the French had made enemies of the Iroquois, and Champlain's Habitation was vulnerable to attack. The colonists didn't have the skills—or the numbers—to defend themselves, and the French king, Louis XIV, was also nervous about the thriving English colonies in America. Determined to keep New France alive, he sent a group of soldiers to boost the fighting power of the colonists.

The soldiers did their job well, and in 1668 the Iroquois agreed to make peace. The regiment prepared to return to France, but the king saw, in all those able-bodied men, a chance to increase the population of his colony and establish a stronger foothold in the New World. He offered free plots of land called seigneuries to any officers who chose to stay. Those who weren't officers were also encouraged to stay and work the seigneuries as tenant farmers.

There was only one problem: now there were six young men in New France for every one woman! Those aren't good numbers when you're trying to grow the population of a settlement.

Once again, the king leapt into action. He decided to invite single and widowed young women to immigrate to New France. His hope was that they would marry the Frenchmen there and start families. But how could anybody persuade women to leave the security and familiarity of their homes for a faraway land with strange foods, harsh winters, the threat of Native attacks, and many other unknown dangers?

The king's advisers decided to recruit beggars and orphans, girls and young women who were already living in deplorable conditions. They offered each girl who would go to New France money from the royal treasury (fifty francs or more, about a year's pay for a common labourer), payable when she married.

The plan was successful. In the 1660s, nearly a thousand hardy, courageous women left France for the New World. Because the program was so strongly supported by the king, these women came to be called *filles du roi,* or "daughters of the king." Although a few did eventually return home, the majority became permanent residents, remaining in New France with their husbands and children for the rest of their lives.

The majority of the *filles du roi* got married and earned their dowry money within a year of their arrival in New France. They were the ancestors of most of today's millions of French Canadians.

Loyal to the Crown

T he English and the French are often called the two founding peoples of Canada. While the French came across the ocean, settling Acadia and establishing the colony of Quebec, many of the earliest English settlers came north from the Thirteen Colonies, fleeing the turmoil of the American Revolution. They were called United Empire Loyalists because they fought alongside the British to keep the American colonies loyal to the Crown.

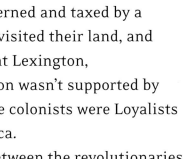

The Seeds of Revolution

Before it boiled over into a full-fledged rebellion, the American Revolution had already been simmering for more than a decade. Many American colonists hated being governed and taxed by a faraway English king who had never even visited their land, and their frustration broke into open warfare at Lexington, Massachusetts, in April 1775. The revolution wasn't supported by everyone, however. At least one-third of the colonists were Loyalists who were against independence for America.

Many Canadians are proud of their Loyalist roots and celebrate them in everything from statues to postage stamps. As many as 4 million Canadians are descended from a Loyalist ancestor.

As the revolt went on, conflict grew between the revolutionaries, called the Patriots, and the Loyalists. The well-organized Patriots wanted to crush local opposition and face England with a united front. They confiscated the Loyalists' weapons and arrested anyone who sympathized with the British cause. Suspected Loyalists were tried in a special court; if found guilty, they faced public floggings or imprisonment.

When frightened Loyalists started to flee their homes, they sought protection from the British troops who'd been sent to prevent the Patriots from gaining independence. Many lived alongside the troops in refugee camps, with little food and shelter. Others banded together into small military units and fought with the British army.

But England soon began to lose the struggle, and the situation grew worse for the Loyalists. Laws were passed to prevent them from buying and selling land, and many were forced to give up their professions. In January 1777, Massachusetts made the "crime" of supporting the British Empire punishable by death. Fearing for their lives, thousands of Loyalists abandoned their homes and fled north to Canada.

Starting Over

The great wave of Loyalists came to Canada in 1783 and 1784. Their homes, property, and old lives were gone, but they were determined to begin again under the British laws they preferred. More than 30,000 headed to Nova Scotia, which then included the territory that is now New Brunswick. Another 8,000 or so went to Quebec and what would become Ontario.

These new immigrants to Canada came from each of the thirteen rebel colonies and all walks of life—lawyers, merchants, farmers, and soldiers. Not all were British. The Loyalists included German, Swiss, and Dutch soldiers who had joined the British army, as well as Natives and black slaves who'd served in support of Britain. They came by wagon, on horseback, or on foot, convinced that they would enjoy a better life under the protection of the Crown.

When great ships brought the Loyalists to Nova Scotia in 1783, some saw only wilderness and rocky soil. But to others, this land was the most beautiful they'd ever encountered.

By 1784, Kingston had already been transformed from a rough Loyalist encampment to a thriving little frontier town.

But the conditions they met were tough. Supplies were scarce, and illness often resulted in death. Before they could even plant their crops, the Loyalists had to devote long, backbreaking hours to clearing the fields and putting up the humble log structures that would be their homes. For some, just the thought of starting over was hard to face. One Loyalist refugee later wrote of watching the ship that had brought her to Nova Scotia sail away. "I climbed to the top of Chipman's Hill," she remembered, " and

Free Land for Newcomers

The British government, eager to shore up its remaining North American colonies, encouraged the Loyalists by offering them free land, which was given out according to a formula based on their service to the Crown. Officers who fought for the British army, for example, received a thousand acres, while privates got a hundred. Those who didn't fight at all also got as much as a hundred acres apiece.

The Loyalists were also promised free transportation to their new property and provisions like farming tools, building materials, blankets, seeds, and food for the first three years of settlement. Immigrants who arrived in spring or summer were housed in tents, bark shelters, or public buildings until they received their land and could build their new homes. Those who arrived by boat in fall or winter lived on the ships until spring came.

This document gave John Hall, a "discharged soldier," the right to sixty acres of land in Sorel, Quebec. Hall had twelve months to "settle and improve the said Lot."

watched the sails disappear, and such a lonely feeling came over me that, although I had not shed a tear through all the war, I sat down on the damp moss with my baby in my lap and cried."

Towards a Great Society

But the Loyalist refugees persevered, and they had a lasting impact on British North America. The population jumped by about a third, and this led directly to the creation of two new territories—New Brunswick in 1784 and Upper Canada (now Ontario) in 1791. Through their numbers alone, the Loyalists helped build a thriving economy, and because many had spent years struggling with the short growing seasons and harsh winters of the Thirteen Colonies, they were already skilled pioneer farmers. They were also optimistic and ambitious, and they saw, in the untouched wilderness, an opportunity to create a great new society.

This 1788 proclamation announces that the province of Quebec has been divided into seven new districts. Four of these would become Upper Canada (now Ontario) in 1791.

Edward Winslow, who moved from New York to Halifax and then the Saint John River in 1783, had the passionate, determined nature that was typical of the Loyalist refugees. "There are assembled here an immense multitude, not of dissolute vagrants such as commonly make the first efforts to settle new countries, but gentlemen of education, farmers formerly independent, and reputable mechanics, who by fortune of war have been deprived of their property," he wrote after his arrival in New Brunswick. "They are as firmly attached to the British constitution as if they never had made a sacrifice.... By Heaven we will be the envy of the American states."

A Loyalist's Story

Hannah Ingraham was just four years old when her father left home to join the British forces and fight against the Americans. She didn't see him again for seven years. When he returned in 1783, he took his family to the safety of the Saint John River valley. In this excerpt, Hannah remembers her mother's struggles and those first brutal months as new Canadians.

Hannah Ingraham in 1860.

We had a comfortable farm, plenty of cows and sheep. But when the war began and he [her father] joined the regulars they [the Americans] took it all away, sold the things, ploughs and all, and my mother was forced to pay rent for her own farm. What father had sown they took away, but what mother raised after she paid rent they let her keep. They took away all our cows and sheep, only let her have one heifer and four sheep....

My father was taken prisoner once but he escaped. The girl who was sent to take him his supper one night told him she would leave the door unbuttoned, and he got off to the woods, but was wandering most two months before he found the army again. Mother was four years without hearing of or from father, whether he was alive or dead; any one would be hanged right up if they were caught bringing letters.

Oh, they were terrible times....

[Father] came home on Sept. 13th, [1783], and said we were to go to Nova Scotia [which then included New Brunswick], that a ship was ready to take us there, so we made all haste to get ready.

We had five wagon loads carried down the Hudson in a sloop and then we went aboard the transport that was to bring us to St. John. I was just eleven years old when we left our farm to come here. It was the last transport for the season, and had in it all those who could not leave sooner....

We lived in a tent at St. Ann's [now Fredericton] till father got a log house raised. He went up through our lot till he found a nice fresh spring of water, he stooped down and pulled away the leaves that were thick over it, and tasted it; it was very good, so there he built his house. We all had rations given us by the Government, flour and butter and pork; and tools were given to the men, too.

One morning when we waked we found the snow lying deep on the ground all around us, and then father came walking through it, and told us the house was ready and not to stop to light a fire then, and not mind the weather, but follow his tracks through the trees, for the trees were so many we soon lost sight of him going up the hill; it was snowing fast, and oh so cold. Father carried a chest and we all carried something and followed him up the hill through the trees.

It was not long before we heard him pounding, and oh what joy to see our gabled end. There was no floor laid, no window, no chimney, no door, but we had a roof at last.

A good fire was blazing on the hearth, and mother had a big loaf of bread with us, and she boiled a kettle of water and put a good piece of butter in a pewter bowl, and we toasted the bread and all sat around the bowl to eat breakfast that morning, and mother said, "Thank God, we are no longer in dread of having shots fired through our house. This is the sweetest meal I have tasted for many a day."

This 1784 Loyalist encampment on the banks of the St. Lawrence River grew into the town of Cornwall, Ontario (then called Johnston). The painting shows people fishing, cooking, and even taking a stroll—anything to pass the time until they received their new land.

North to Freedom

Of the 30,000 Loyalists who came north to Nova Scotia in 1783 and 1784, roughly 10 per cent, or 3,000, were black. Many of the white Loyalists brought their black slaves north with them, and they continued to serve their masters in Canada. Other blacks, however, had escaped from their owners to fight in the British army, and they came to Canada to claim the freedom and land grants they had been promised in exchange for their military service. Slaves or free, these pioneering men and women were important founders of this nation.

But life was not easy for them. Many black Loyalists never got their land grants, and those who did were hardly better off. The parcels they were offered were usually ones no other Loyalists wanted. They had poor soil or rocks or were still covered in thick forest. No amount of backbreaking work could ever transform these tracts into fields that might one day produce thriving crops.

This proclamation from the governor of Virginia encouraged black slaves to fight for the British army during the American Revolution. In it, the Earl of Dunmore declares that "all indented Servants, Negroes, or others" will become free when they "bear Arms [and join] His Majesty's Troops."

By His Excellency the Right Honorable JOHN Earl of DUNMORE, His Majesty's Lieutenant and Governor General of the Colony and Dominion of Virginia, and Vice Admiral of the same.

A PROCLAMATION.

As I have ever entertained Hopes, that an Accommodation might have taken Place between GREAT-BRITAIN and this Colony, without being compelled by my Duty to this most disagreeable but now absolutely necessary Step, rendered so by a Body of armed Men unlawfully assembled, firing on His Majesty's Tenders, and the formation of an Army, and that Army now on their March to attack His Majesty's Troops and destroy the well disposed Subjects of this Colony. To defeat such treasonable Purposes, and that all such Traitors, and their Abettors, may be brought to Justice, and that the Peace, and good Order of this Colony may be again restored, which the ordinary Course of the Civil Law is unable to effect; I have thought fit to issue this my Proclamation, hereby declaring, that until the aforesaid good Purposes can be obtained, I do in Virtue of the Power and Authority to ME given, by His Majesty, determine to execute Martial Law, and cause the same to be executed throughout this Colony: and to the end that Peace and good Order may the sooner be restored, I do require every Person capable of bearing Arms, to resort to His Majesty's STANDARD, or be looked upon as Traitors to His Majesty's Crown and Government, and thereby become liable to the Penalty the Law inflicts upon such Offences; such as forfeiture of Life, confiscation of Lands, &c. &c. And I do hereby further declare all indented Servants, Negroes, or others, (appertaining to Rebels,) free that are able and willing to bear Arms, they joining His Majesty's Troops as soon as may be, for the more speedily reducing this Colony to a proper Sense of their Duty, to His Majesty's Crown and Dignity. I do further order, and require, all His Majesty's Leige Subjects, to retain their Quitrents, or any other Taxes due or that may become due, in their own Custody, till such Time as Peace may be again restored to this at present most unhappy Country, or demanded of them for their former salutary Purposes, by Officers properly authorised to receive the same.

GIVEN under my Hand on board the Ship WILLIAM, off NORFOLK, the 7th Day of NOVEMBER, in the SIXTEENTH Year of His Majesty's Reign.

DUNMORE.

(GOD save the KING.)

And what about the other resources promised by the British—the lumber, the money, the tools? Again, the black Loyalists were always at the end of the line. Many suffered through their first winters in the inadequate temporary structures they put up just for shelter, but then they weren't given the money and materials they needed to start fresh in the spring and construct more solid buildings.

Simply put, the black Loyalists were not treated like their white counterparts, despite all the promises. Many had to work clearing roads and cutting trees for the British to earn the same rations that were given to white Loyalists for free. It was a hard life, but the black Loyalists managed to come together and build several strong communities of their own. These were bolstered by later waves of black migrants, especially those who came in the wake of the War of 1812. Many also came north from America when the British Parliament passed several bills restricting slavery throughout the British Empire, which included Canada. They all saw their chance for a better life.

The black Loyalists mostly lived together in their own separate communities. At its height, the one at Birchtown, near Shelburne, Nova Scotia, was the largest settlement of freed blacks outside of Africa.

This black family walks along a road just outside Halifax in about 1835. They may have been among the 2,000 or more blacks who came to Canada for land and freedom after the War of 1812.

The Underground Railroad was run by white and freed black "conductors." They transported hidden slaves by wagons or carts through a series of "stations," or safe houses, to freedom in Canada.

The Underground Railroad

These people were only the first in a long line of blacks who came north to freedom. They were joined, perhaps most famously, by the passengers of the Underground Railroad in the mid-1800s. This secret network helped as many as 30,000 black slaves escape to Canada, where slavery had finally been abolished in 1834. The numbers grew after 1850, when American fugitive slave laws gave owners the right to track down and arrest runaway slaves anywhere in the United States.

Those who made it successfully to Canada found freedom but often little else. Few white Canadians treated their black neighbours as equals. Blacks were barred from hotels and churches, and many whites refused to allow black children to attend the same public schools as their own children. If that wasn't bad enough, many blacks feared they would be captured and returned to their former owners in the United States.

Yet blacks continued to immigrate to Canada. In some parts of the country, they were valued for the many skills they had acquired—as gunsmiths, barbers, and labourers, for example—and they became respected members of their communities. Soon, Canada had its first black doctors, lawyers, and teachers. Mary Ann Shadd Cary, a former slave, started the first integrated school in Canada and became the first black woman in North America to edit a newspaper. Canada still had its drawbacks, but freedom was guaranteed and there was hope for a better future.

And so, blacks kept on coming. In 1858, many hundreds of black gold-seekers left California and migrated north to British Columbia, and around 1910, black farmers from Oklahoma started moving to Saskatchewan, Manitoba, and Alberta. These new Canadians were fed up with American laws that wouldn't allow them to vote, own property, or have access to education.

A prosperous-looking black family poses in Vulcan, Alberta, in the early 1900s.

The next major wave of blacks came to Canada in the 1960s and 1970s. In 1960, the Canadian government adopted a Bill of Rights that banned discrimination. Canada's black population doubled, with most newcomers arriving from the islands of the Caribbean and from Africa. Now about 8 per cent of all new Canadians come from these lands.

Today, there are about half a million black Canadians—people who've come here from countries all over the world. Although they first settled largely in the Maritimes, blacks now live mostly in Canada's cities. They celebrate their culture with holidays like Kwanzaa and with Toronto's annual Caribana festival, and they remember their heritage every February during Black History Month. Given their more than 400 years of service to this country, that's a long, proud history to recall.

KEEP THE NEGRO ACROSS THE LINE

THE WINNIPEG BOARD OF TRADE TAKES DECIDED ACTION

Not Good Settlers or Agreeable Neighbors Either

Winnipeg, Man., April 19.—The Winnipeg board of trade this evening passed a strongly worded resolution, which will be forwarded to Ottawa, condemning the admission of negroes into Canada as settlers.

It is set forth in the resolution that these new-comers are not successful farmers nor agreeable neighbors for white settlers. The board also passed a resolution similar to that of the Manufacturers' association on the proposal to amend the railway act to enable the railway commission to suspend railway tariffs or charges on appeals from patrons of the railways against which grievances are held.

Black farmers who immigrated to the prairies in the 1910s still faced discrimination, as this newspaper article shows.

Champlain's Right-Hand Man

Mathieu da Costa was a daring adventurer and traveller. Born in West Africa, he made his way to Portugal and then came to the shores of the New World as an interpreter for Samuel de Champlain in 1605. Because he spoke both Mi'kmaq and French, da Costa was able to bridge the linguistic and cultural gaps between the explorers and the local Natives. He was probably the first black to set foot on the land that would one day be Canada.

The Lost Town of Africville

Thousands of black American slaves who had supported the British during the American Revolution came to Nova Scotia in search of land, freedom, and equality. Although they didn't quite find what they were looking for, they did quickly establish many thriving black communities, especially in the areas around Halifax, Shelburne, and eventually Guysborough.

One of the most successful of these communities was Halifax's Africville. Founded in the mid-1800s by families who'd grown tired of working their rocky, thin-soiled lands for little gain, Africville grew to include about 400 hard-working, tight-knit residents. Allied in their common struggle to feed themselves and their children, pay their taxes, and combat the racism that made surviving an even greater struggle, the residents drew on one another for strength. They came together to build a church, a school, and even their own post office.

This certificate of freedom gave Cato Ramsay the right to go to Nova Scotia, "or wherever else he may think proper."

Africville thrived for about 150 years. But Halifax's white community had little regard for it. While the city grew and prospered, gaining electricity, water and sewage services, and paved roads, Africville was neglected. In fact, Halifax made Africville home to a prison, a hospital for infectious diseases, a slaughterhouse, and a garbage dump. When residents asked for the services that existed everywhere else, the city council refused.

How does a neighbourhood remain united when it's faced with such racism? "We found ways to survive the discrimination," said Irvine Carvery, head of the Africville

NEW-YORK, 21st April 1783.

THIS is to certify to whomsoever it may concern, that the Bearer hereof Cato Ramsay a Negro, resorted to the British Lines, in consequence of the Proclamations of Sir William Howe, and Sir Henry Clinton, late Commanders in Chief in America; and that the said Negro has hereby his Excellency Sir Guy Carleton's Permission to go to Nova-Scotia, or wherever else he may think proper.

By Order of Brigadier General Birch,

Residents had to pump water by hand just to be able to cook or keep themselves clean. But they were proud of Africville and what it represented.

Africville was the dumping ground for Halifax's least desirable institutions and businesses. There was even a railway line right through the middle of the neighbourhood.

Genealogy Society. "Our resolve and our strength came from our strong religious beliefs. This held people together during those very difficult times."

But one day in the 1960s, the end came. Halifax city officials decided to demolish the community. Residents were offered money to leave their homes, but those who refused to go were simply evicted. Bulldozers came during the night, and personal belongings were moved to public housing complexes in the back of dump trucks. The community that African Canadians had built and loved for more than a century and a half was destroyed.

In 2002, the spot where Africville once stood was named a National Historic Site. But to the former residents, it's not enough. Some are still seeking compensation for their land and for the destruction of their community and businesses. "Many people believed that when the physical structure and buildings of Africville were gone, the spirit would die," said Carvery. "But it hasn't died. Instead of dying away, in fact, the community, and the unity around the community, has grown…. The people of Africville still speak with a common voice."

From Island to New Land

The Irish have been coming to Canada since the 1600s. Like so many other immigrants, they left their homeland for the opportunities of the New World, sailing across the sea to Newfoundland to work at the fishing stations and coming north for free land as part of the Loyalist migration of the 1780s. But like the black Loyalists, they didn't always get a warm welcome. For most of their history, in fact, the Irish have struggled against prejudice and discrimination, even as they made a lasting impact on their adopted home.

The cholera outbreak of the 1830s terrified Canadians and took thousands of lives. In this painting, the sky is black with smoke as frightened Quebecers try to fumigate their city.

Leaving the Emerald Isle

Ireland is a lush place of green rolling hills and beautiful farmland, but it has a stormy history of uprisings and rebellions, famines and other natural disasters. This was what prompted about half a million Irish to abandon their island home in the decades leading up to 1850. In what was the largest migration from any one country up to that point, they headed for what they hoped would be the more welcoming shores of British North America. Once there, some went south to major American cities like New York and Boston, but many settled in the Maritimes and Upper and Lower Canada. Most of those who came preferred to work as labourers for others, instead of farming their own land. They scratched out modest lives in port cities like Halifax, Saint John, and Quebec.

But if times were tough in the New World, things were even worse back home. Cholera swept Ireland in 1832, killing 25,000 people, and in 1845 disease hit the potato crop, wiping out the island's primary source of food. Suddenly, poor Irish families could not grow enough healthy potatoes to feed themselves. They began to starve. When the potato crop failed again the next year, and once more in 1848, the death toll mounted. Almost a million Irish would eventually die in what came to be known as the Great Potato Famine. Another 2 million desperate people would leave the Emerald Isle as part of a dramatic mass migration, with as many as 400,000 coming to Canada.

This 1832 quarantine questionnaire was designed to root out sick immigrants. This crossing was mercifully free of disease, however. One infant passenger was lost to teething, and a sailor fell overboard and was drowned.

Aboard the Coffin Ships

Cholera, famine ... and now another deadly disease struck. As the starving refugees fled across the ocean, packed into cramped, rickety ships that were never meant to carry passengers, typhus appeared. The overcrowded, filthy vessels, nicknamed "coffin ships," created the perfect conditions for this killer disease, one of the most contagious of all. Spread by lice, typhus thrived in the dank holds of the ships, quickly infecting people who were already weakened by malnutrition and starvation. As many as 8,000 immigrants took their last breath amid the stench of these awful vessels and then were quietly slipped over the side.

Panic seized the harbours of British North America as the first spring ships of 1847 brought typhus to their towns and cities. To try to contain the disease, officials at Quebec City diverted 398 ships to Grosse-Ile, a deserted island in the St. Lawrence River that had been turned into a quarantine station. About 4,500 corpses were removed from the ships when they docked, and another 5,424 people died on the island and are buried there to this day.

The survivors were allowed to leave Grosse-Ile only when the quarantine period was up and they'd been given a clean bill of health. After two to three months at sea and

Grosse-Ile has a monument to the Irish typhus victims. It's a Celtic cross, a traditional Irish symbol of heaven and earth and the cycle of life.

Monsieur O'Reilly?

Hundreds of Irish children had been orphaned by typhus by the time they finally left Grosse-Ile and were allowed to set foot on the mainland. Fortunately, many kind-hearted Quebec families were waiting to welcome them into their farmhouses and cottages. The first few months must have been difficult for these frightened, lonely children, who were in a strange land and did not understand the language of their new French families. But they were allowed to keep their Irish names, out of respect for their heritage and their deceased parents. Even today, Quebec is home to many proud French-speaking O'Reillys, O'Sheas, and Sullivans, the direct descendants of those original young Irish immigrants.

These immigrants are patiently awaiting their medical exams. If they show any signs of disease at all, they will need to be quarantined on Grosse-Ile until they are well again.

possibly another several weeks in quarantine, they were finally able to travel on to Quebec and Montreal, Kingston and Toronto. But what they found there was discrimination, fear, and mistrust. The Irish had become linked in many Canadians' minds with poverty and disease.

Outside of Quebec, where Irish Catholics found a relatively warm welcome, no one wanted to hire them for anything more than the lowest-paying jobs. But many Irish, frantic to feed their families and keep a roof over their heads, took whatever they could get. Others gave up on the towns and headed to the lumber camps, where they worked hard for slim wages and at least managed to find shelter in the shantytowns that sprang up alongside the work sites.

Through hard work, perseverance, and determination, the Irish built the better life they had been seeking all along. They overcame the many obstacles that were laid in their paths and made important, lasting contributions to Canadian life. Today, about one in ten Canadians proudly claim Irish descent. But they aren't the only ones who celebrate the Emerald Isle. Every March 17, on St. Patrick's Day, Canadians of all backgrounds join in the fun, proof that, in this country, the shamrock is now intertwined with the maple leaf.

Quarantine Island

Grosse-Ile's one ambulance stands poised and ready for action. The island was severely understaffed, and six men were employed to do nothing but dig graves every day.

The quarantine station at Grosse-Ile was built in 1832 to prevent the spread of cholera into Lower Canada. Immigrants arriving by ship who showed any signs of illness were sent there to wait out the disease's incubation period—anywhere from a few days to a few weeks.

When the typhus-filled "coffin ships" began arriving in early 1847, the station had room for 150 patients. But with so many ships docking each day, it was soon dangerously overcrowded. Shanties were hastily erected, and sails and spars from the boats were used to make temporary shelters. Those who were already sick were put into "fever sheds," with only straw for bedding. When someone died, the straw was often not even disinfected before another patient was brought in. Many healthy families, trying to stay that way, chose to sleep on the shore rather than risk infection in the shelters.

There were not nearly enough attendants to care for all the sick, and sometimes desperately ill patients spent all night sleeping beside the bodies of the dead. Confusion spread, and soon the ships at anchor themselves became miniature quarantine stations, holding the sick, the dying, and even the already dead alongside those who were healthy.

This second-class hotel was only one of several that were eventually built on the island. They offered more comfortable accommodations to those who were well.

In 1847 alone, 68,106 immigrants were examined at Grosse-Ile. At the height of the typhus outbreak, more than a hundred bodies were being buried each day. Hundreds of frightened Irish children were orphaned, and many doctors, priests, and nuns who'd come to tend the sick also fell victim to the disease. In that one year, more than 5,000 quarantine patients died.

For decades, Grosse-Ile remained the point of arrival for most immigrants who sailed across the Atlantic Ocean for the eastern shores of Canada. As medical knowledge increased, however, it became a better, safer place to pass through. A greater understanding of how disease spread led to new methods for dealing with infected immigrants. The island was divided into sections to keep the sick apart from the healthy. A laboratory was set up to make testing quicker and easier. And ships and baggage were disinfected to keep any outbreaks under control.

By 1923, there were fewer immigrants coming to Canada, so those who needed treatment were sent to a hospital built in Quebec City. A few years later, Grosse-Ile was shut down. In 1984, the island was recognized as a National Historic Site. Today, visitors can see the historic buildings, the burial grounds, and the memorials that honour the thousands of immigrants who entered Canada through this forlorn spot.

Built in the 1850s, the Old Wash House was the building where the immigrants' clothes were cleaned and disinfected, which helped control the spread of disease.

Going West

I've Been Working on the Railroad

When new arrivals like the Irish docked in eastern Canada in the early 1800s, they usually settled nearby. Travelling farther west was extremely difficult because there was no railway linking the coasts of the country. In fact, Canada's one western province, British Columbia, was effectively cut off from the rest of the nation, a situation that was causing headaches for politicians from one coast to the other. British Columbia, after all, had agreed to join Confederation only because the government had promised to link the country with a transcontinental rail line within ten years. By 1880, nine years had passed—and Canada was running out of time to fulfil its promise.

This image of Donald A. Smith, a major backer of the Canadian Pacific Railway, driving home the Last Spike is one of the most famous photographs in Canadian history. But the Chinese labourers who actually laid much of the western track are nowhere to be seen.

Desperate, Sir Charles Tupper, the minister of railways, turned to Andrew Onderdonk, an American contractor and engineer, and asked him to build the section of the Canadian Pacific Railway from Port Moody, on the Pacific coast, to Craigellachie, where the Last Spike would be driven home. This involved laying track through hundreds of kilometres of the most dangerous, difficult terrain in the country. Onderdonk realized immediately that he would never find enough local men to do the job, so he decided to import workers from China.

When Onderdonk announced his plan, the people of British Columbia reacted angrily. They didn't think it was fair for foreigners to take jobs from Canadians—even though this was dangerous work that no Canadian wanted to do—and they were nervous about living alongside people from another country. But Onderdonk stood firm. If he was not permitted to recruit Chinese workers, he warned, the rail line would take twelve more years to complete!

In the end, the government gave him the go-ahead. Between 1881 and 1885, 17,000 Chinese labourers made the enormous decision to leave their homes and families and cross the sea to Canada.

A Dollar a Day

The voyage across the Pacific Ocean to British Columbia took fifty long days. When the Chinese labourers arrived, there was no time to recover or to adjust to their new surroundings. They were put right to work, toiling away high up the sides of mountain valleys, where one wrong step could start a rock slide or even plunge them to their death. In this perilous environment, they had to clear the roadbed of the railway, secure the rail ties with gravel, and use sledgehammers and chisels to carve out rock from tunnel walls and overhangs. Worse yet, they were expected to position the nitroglycerin charges used to blast out sections of mountainside. The liquid nitroglycerin was unpredictable and more dangerous than dynamite. Even the most careful workers risked being caught in a blast or crushed in one of the massive rock slides the explosions always set off.

When the Canadian Pacific Railway was finally finished, it did exactly what it was supposed to— unite the country from one end to the other.

The Chinese workers lived in ramshackle shanties set up beside the dirt, noise, and mess of the railway tracks.

The Chinese didn't get much in return for all their hard work and courage. They were paid as little as a dollar a day, half the amount that white workers earned. They had inadequate medical care, even though the work they were doing and the conditions they lived in made them prone to injuries, disease, and exhaustion. Is it any wonder that about 4,000 Chinese workers died before the railway was finished in 1885?

Life wasn't much better for those who survived. Few even came close to earning enough money to return home, and those who stayed had to remain alone. Why? In 1885, the very year the railway was completed and the workers lost their usefulness, the government passed the Chinese Immigration Act. This law said that every Chinese person who wanted to enter the country had to pay a head tax, or entry tax, of fifty dollars. This was a large amount of money in the 1880s, much more than the average Chinese person could afford to pay.

Once the railway was completed and the workers no longer needed, the government began forcing new Chinese immigrants to pay an expensive head tax.

The Exclusion Act

Just as it was meant to, the head tax kept out most new Chinese immigrants, along with the family members of those who were already here. But over time, the population did slowly begin to increase again. Many white Canadians were alarmed by this. So on July 1, 1923, which the Chinese began to refer to as Humiliation Day, the government acted, passing the Chinese Exclusion Act.

All these obstacles seemed only to make the Chinese more committed to their adopted home, however. In the Second World War, loyal Chinese Canadians served as soldiers, nurses, and pilots, defending the country they loved. In time, anti-Asian feelings began to decline. In 1947, Chinese Canadians gained the right to vote in federal elections and the Exclusion Act was finally repealed. The wives and children of men already in Canada rushed to reunite their families, and Chinese immigrants have arrived in great numbers ever since.

The caption to this 1879 political cartoon has the white British Columbian telling his Chinese neighbour exactly why he so dislikes him: "You won't drink whiskey, and talk politics and vote like us."

Today, Chinese Canadians pass on to their children the language and traditions of their ancestral home, and they share stories with them too—stories of their forebears' journey to Canada, of their struggle to earn a living and carve a new identity in an unfamiliar land. Those stories are now woven into the fabric of Canadian history. And Canada has finally honoured the work that those thousands of Chinese labourers did on the railway. Now they are remembered in a monument at the foot of Toronto's CN Tower, with the railway tracks still stretching out in the distance behind. This statue of two men laying wooden railway track at a dangerous height is testament to the bold and important role the Chinese played in linking this country from coast to coast.

Spotlight on

Canada's Chinatowns

Many Chinese started businesses like restaurants. They could serve their fellow Chinese Canadians even if they couldn't speak English well.

When the Canadian Pacific Railway was finally completed, thousands of Chinese men found themselves out of work. The few who could afford to returned to China. But most stayed in British Columbia or headed towards the towns and cities of the prairies and eastern Canada. It must have been an unpleasant experience. Because they looked different and came from a country that no one knew much about, the Chinese had a hard time finding jobs and places to live. Many people would simply have given up, but these were men who had faced landslides, explosions, disease, and fatigue. They would make their own jobs and build their own success.

What kind of work could they do, however, when they had so little? Many Chinese started businesses like laundries and restaurants that were in demand but didn't require much initial money or a great ability to speak English. While the businesses soon began to prosper, it didn't make most Canadians treat the Chinese any better. They were pelted with rocks on the street, refused adequate health care, and denied the right to vote in some provinces. Attacks on Chinese businesses were not uncommon.

Victoria was home to Canada's first Chinatown—a chaotic neighbourhood of flimsy homes that looked like they wouldn't survive a strong gust of wind. Today, it's a National Historic Site.

Very quickly, the Chinese learned that if they were going to survive and flourish, they needed to band together and support one another with shelter, services, and even simple conversation. This sparked the growth of Chinese neighbourhoods—or "Chinatowns"—in several cities, most notably Victoria, Vancouver, and Toronto.

These Chinatowns were life-savers for men who—because of the head tax— were unable to bring over their wives and children. Those who lived and worked in Chinese neighbourhoods could speak their own language and find support from people who were sharing the same experience. Together, the Chinese preserved their heritage. They also founded organizations to help those who were new to the community.

Slowly, most Chinatowns grew bigger and more prosperous. And when Chinese women and children were finally allowed to enter Canada, they became communities that families could share. Today, there are more than ten Chinatowns in Canada, with some cities home to several. Toronto has six of its own, and their combined population is half a million. All those Chinatowns are an important part of Canada's cultural landscape, and the Chinese are today one of the country's most active and dynamic immigrant groups.

Thousands of tourists travel to Victoria's Chinatown each year to see sites like the Gates of Harmonious Interest and the world's narrowest street, Fan Tan Alley.

Velkomin

I n 1872, just after British Columbia joined Confederation on the promise of a trans-continental railway, Sigtryggur Jónasson set sail for Canada. He would be the first Icelander to set foot on this land since the Norse explorers in the tenth and eleventh centuries.

Jónasson's faraway island home was plagued by disease, famine, severe winters, and devastating volcanic eruptions that spewed ash, destroying homes and pastureland. When people in Iceland read Jónasson's enthusiastic letters describing the beauty of Ontario, they were convinced to join him. Most came reluctantly, for they fiercely loved their homeland, but they hoped to start a colony that would be a "new" Iceland, a place where they could stay together, speak their language, keep their customs, and prosper. They were able to leave the soil of Iceland behind because they knew they were taking its spirit with them.

This contract guaranteed the Stefansson family—father, mother, and four children under twelve—passage to Canada. When they got to New Iceland, Johann Stefansson and his wife, Ingibjorg Johannesdottir, had at least one more child—the future Arctic explorer Vilhjalmur Stefansson.

Landfall at Willow Point

Sigtryggur Jónasson was just twenty when he became the first modern-day Icelander to travel to Canada. He came to be known as the Father of New Iceland.

Jónasson wanted to find just the right place for this Icelandic colony. Eventually the federal government sent him and two other Icelanders on a trip west to the unsettled wilderness of what is now Manitoba. When the men arrived on the west shore of Lake Winnipeg, they found fertile soil, abundant fish, and forests for timber and fuel. They had found their new home.

In 1875, 235 hardy Icelanders picked up and moved west. These bold adventurers arrived at Willow Point, near what is now Gimli, on October 21 of that year. They set up tents, built shelters for several families to share, and even raised a school that first winter. They were so determined to make their mark, in fact, that they had convinced the government to let them have an Icelandic reserve on this unsurveyed Canadian soil. Their settlement would have its own constitution and laws, as well as its own council to administer them. It would be called Nyja Island, or New Iceland.

In 1875, more than 200 Icelandic men, women, and children travelled along the Red River from Winnipeg and landed at Willow Point. There was no room for the large group on Lake Winnipeg's only steamer, so they made their way there on dangerous, hard-to-steer flat-bottomed boats.

Steep Rock Man

The fishing industry was a very important part of the success of New Iceland, although the settlers, whose nets were made for deep-sea fishing, at first had trouble bringing in any catch. Eventually they learned to adapt their skills, however, and fish became the colony's staple product.

The first few winters in New Iceland were very tough. But the Icelanders were even tougher. Some had never even seen a tree, and yet they had to clear many acres of land! They figured out how to hunt, how to handle unfamiliar tools, and how to grow wheat on the new land. The women learned how to cook meals with the foods that were available to them, using sweet sap for sugar and wheat kernels for coffee. They didn't get their first two cows until the spring of 1876.

Jónasson, meanwhile, returned home to Iceland and encouraged others to join the new colony. Almost 1,200 more came in 1876. It was easier for this second group because they were helped by those who'd gone before. But when smallpox struck that fall, it hit hard, spreading like wildfire throughout New Iceland. And more disasters followed— floods, scarlet fever, diphtheria, and measles. Many of the newcomers abandoned their colony for Winnipeg, and by 1881, the population of New Iceland had fallen to 250. But others just couldn't give up. Culture, language, and determination held them together and eventually attracted more new Icelandic immigrants.

The Day of the Icelanders

By 1900, the population of New Iceland had blossomed to 2,000, and Winnipeg had an Icelandic population of 4,000. Today, there are about 180,000 Canadians of Icelandic descent. They have never forgotten their ties to their ancestral island home, and many thousands journey to Gimli every year to celebrate Islendingadagurinn, or the Day of the Icelanders, Manitoba's annual Icelandic festival.

Many modern Icelandic Canadians still enjoy telling Old World tales, which often reflect a strong belief in superstition. Some are convinced that Icelandic settlers even brought ghosts with them to Canada. It is said that Icelanders would sometimes send family ghosts to harass difficult neighbours. These ghosts would stay with their host families for generations, moving with them from farm to farm and even from country to country. Legend has it that one famous ghost made his way to Canada in just this fashion, having been carried across the ocean by his unsuspecting host with all his other treasured belongings!

First celebrated in 1890, Canada's Day of the Icelanders is now an annual tradition with people of Icelandic descent from all over the world. Some really get into the spirit—dressing in authentic-looking Viking outfits and taking part in mock battlefield skirmishes.

Come to Canada!

How do you make sure everyone knows your land belongs to you? You live on it, of course. That's what the Canadian government believed, anyway. So in 1870, when the vast and mostly unsettled North-Western Territory (which stretched from Ontario to British Columbia and north to the Arctic Ocean) was transferred to Canada by the Hudson's Bay Company, Prime Minister John A. Macdonald began encouraging people to move there to live.

When the government realized there weren't enough Canadians to go around, it began trying to attract settlers by offering free land to farmers in Britain, northern Europe, and the United States. Posters like this Swedish one were designed to contradict the view most Europeans had of this country as a cold and wild place. Here, a content farm worker who looks familiarly northern European gathers wheat from a gently rolling field.

Agents were sent overseas to try to entice immigrants. The government paid representatives to tour the countryside in horse-drawn carts or in exhibition wagons decorated with promotional illustrations. They gave lectures, showed slides, and handed out brochures that advertised the country. This "Girl from Canada," with her flag-adorned dress and her cheerfully festooned bicycle, might not have convinced many to emigrate, but she certainly is attention-grabbing!

Canadian government officials weren't the only ones pumping money and energy into advertising the Canadian West. Many large transportation companies, including railway and steamship lines, were encouraging immigration as well. After all, the more people travelled, the more their services would be used! When the Canadian Pacific Railway was completed in 1885, the company began using brochures, decals, and posters to advertise for immigrants to come and ride the rails to their new life.

This early 1900s Canadian Pacific Railway steamship poster is written entirely in the Cyrillic alphabet. It showed would-be immigrants, perhaps from Ukraine, what the inside of a CPR ship was like, from the long white tables of the dining room to the cramped quarters of a typical cabin.

Canadian atlases were translated into different languages and then given out to schoolchildren. When the atlases came home with the students, the parents might peek inside, examine the maps, admire the attractive pictures of the Canadian landscape—and see the names and addresses of Canadian immigration offices. This was a subtle way to sneak past the advertising restrictions that many countries put in place to try to keep their hard-working farmers from being tempted away to other lands.

"*Lees dit!*" this poster commands. "Read this!" Many Dutch farmers must have done just that—and been persuaded to come to Manitoba. Between 1890 and 1930, about 25,000 Dutch immigrants entered Canada and headed west. Many also moved north from the United States, where good, inexpensive land was becoming difficult to find.

Ties That Bind

Icelanders were not the only ones who began to look across the ocean for a better life. In 1891, two Ukrainian farmers, concerned about the poverty of their homeland, headed off to try their luck in Alberta. They had heard that the Canadian government was giving away parcels of free land, and they were convinced that Alberta would be a place of opportunity for them and their fellow farmers.

But it still was not going to be easy. Those who owned land in Ukraine had to sell it just to pay for the ocean passage. They could bring with them only as much as they could carry—perhaps some handmade tools, some seeds to plant in Canadian soil, a wool quilt or handwoven blanket, and a few religious pictures. They had to look ahead to a future they could hardly imagine, with no house, no animals, and not much food until they were able to grow some themselves.

The ocean voyage alone sometimes took a month—an unpleasantly rough thirty days, in most cases—and when the travellers landed in Halifax, they still faced an endless train

Canada was often promoted as a land of bright sunshine, crisp blue skies, and abundant fields of wheat stretching as far as the eye could see.

CANADA WEST

CANADA ~ The New Homeland

These Ukrainian pioneers posed with their six small children at a train station in Quebec. They were probably just about to board one of the colonist cars for the long journey west. In the background, a sign advertises a full meal for just a quarter.

ride west. Most would board one of the so-called colonist cars, which were added to many trains expressly for these new settlers. Five hundred or more adults and children would spend five or six long days chugging along in these cars, their few possessions at their feet as they crowded together on bare wooden benches that converted into sleeping berths at night. To help pass the time, passengers would chat, exchange farming tips and recipes, and share dreams and fears. And so a sense of togetherness was born.

Home at Last

When the train arrived at their final destination, the immigrants had to get busy right away. Before they could even begin to face the challenges of learning a new language or familiarizing themselves with unusual foods and customs, they had to think about finding somewhere to live. They knew the Canadian government wanted to encourage

A Saskatchewan farmer stands proudly in front of his neat little whitewashed house.

This 1893 receipt from the Dominion Lands office was proof that this settler had paid his fee and was entitled to a lot of land somewhere near Calgary.

Strength in Numbers

Many Ukrainians decided to choose lots near one another, even if that meant some would end up with poor-quality land. The importance of being close to relatives, friends, and fellow villagers from back home often outweighed the desire for a superior lot. Having neighbours who were sharing the same hardships and struggles helped lift the spirits. And homesteaders looked out for one another too. Established pioneers often hosted newly arrived families and helped them build their first Canadian homes.

settlement in the West and was offering free or inexpensive homesteads to anyone who would come and farm the prairies. In Alberta, settlers were simply required to pay a small fee, build a house, clear about a fifth of their property, and then farm it. The home-steaders had to live there for at least six months for three consecutive years. Once they'd done all that, the land was theirs for good.

To choose their lots, the new Canadians would head to the homestead office and study a map of the local area. Of course, it was impossible to tell from a map what the land would actually be like. With a deep breath, they would choose the piece of property that would be theirs, hoping for fertile soil. In later years, homesteaders were often just randomly assigned land by the immigration officers who'd lured them to Canada.

A Century Apart

Just three years after those first two farmers came west in 1891, there were several thousand Ukrainians in communities stretching from Winnipeg to

Edmonton. In fact, in the years between the 1890s and the beginning of the First World War, about 170,000 Ukrainians settled in Canada. Until the 1930s, three-quarters of them lived in rural communities and worked as farmers. But others moved from their farms to nearby towns or cities, and many thriving Ukrainian neighbourhoods soon sprang up in these urban centres.

Today, over a million people consider themselves Ukrainian Canadians. Each year, thousands enjoy the National Ukrainian Festival in Dauphin, Manitoba, the largest celebration of Ukrainian culture in North America. There, people eat traditional foods, including kolbassa (a spicy sausage) and borscht (a beet soup), listen to folk groups and modern Ukrainian bands, and compete in music competitions. But you don't have to attend that three-day event to get a taste of the culture. Most modern Ukrainian Canadians have made a deliberate effort to maintain Old World traditions, for they believe strongly that shared rituals and a common language preserve the ties between families, friends, and neighbours.

Ukrainians are good at keeping old bonds strong and building new ones. That's what allowed them to leave behind the only home they'd ever known for a land they'd never seen, to forge new ties and create a new life, and to shape their adopted home into a country where people from all backgrounds and all walks of life are welcomed.

The painter William Kurelek was greatly influenced by his Ukrainian heritage. This piece was one of a series that told the story of Ukrainian farmers coming to Canada.

Spotlight on

A First Canadian Home

Ukrainians have always believed strongly in lending a helping hand. Here, seasoned homesteaders help a newcomer build his first Canadian home.

When the Ukrainians arrived on the prairies, their most immediate task was to build a house. Those who came to an area that other Ukrainians had already settled were lucky and would often be put up by friends, family members, or even former fellow villagers while they built their own solid homes. Others built temporary structures for shelter while they worked on their permanent cabins.

All homesteaders had to work quickly and carefully. First, they would choose a good site for the house—a spot, for example, where the trees were already thin—and then they would clear the land, keeping as many logs as possible to build with. They would peel the bark from the logs, notch out each end so they fitted snugly together, and put them in place. On one wall, space was left for a wide chimney of stone, and holes were cut for doors and windows. To hold the logs together—and keep out freezing winter winds—

This little Ukrainian home has seen many harsh winters. Its whitewashing has begun to chip away, exposing the log beams underneath, and one corner seems to be sinking into the ground.

the settlers made a kind of plaster with clay they dug from their own soil and mixed with water and grass. With the plaster, they filled the space between the logs.

If they had time, the settlers would make a paint. They would gather limestone rocks from the fields and burn them over hot fires to extract a powdery chemical called lime, mixing this with water. Then they painted this whitewash over top of the plaster to give their home a clean appearance. Finally, they would pile earth low against the log walls for added insulation. If planks from the local sawmill were available, they used them to make a roof. Otherwise, they thatched a roof with straw.

Building a house and furnishing it could cost $500 to $1,500. (This was at a time when a lumberhand working from dawn to dusk earned just $35 to $50 a month.) Other items were costly, too. A plough might be $14, a wagon $20, a cow $30, and a yoke of oxen $180. Any money the homesteaders had scraped together to bring to Canada was usually quickly spent. As a result, many could not afford to wait for the income that their own crops would bring only after several months of growing time. Once their homes were built, the men often had to leave their families to earn extra cash working on the railway or at a more prosperous farm. It was hard on everyone, but the families did their best to stick together. Eventually, their homesteads became homes, their fields were sowed, and their lives took root in the new land.

These settlers show off their traditional Ukrainian dress.

By Hook or by Crook

The Italians had been promised jobs and a place to live. Many ended up in primitive construction camps like this one deep in the Rocky Mountains.

When they first began trying to attract people to Canada with the offer of free land in the west, government agents had focused their efforts on northern and eastern Europeans, like Ukrainians. They had deliberately avoided encouraging southern Europeans. At the time, many Canadians believed that people from countries like Italy were unreliable and didn't work hard—and therefore were not suitable for Canada.

These were the late 1800s, however. There was a railway to build, and many new companies were popping up. Everyone needed labourers—as many as they could get, from anywhere they were available. The managers of the Canadian Pacific Railway had already imported men from China, and now they were hoping to lure desperate workers from other countries as well. Owners of construction companies, mines, and factories were equally eager for whatever cheap labour they could find.

They began to turn their attention to Italy. Economic conditions were bad there, and unskilled young men were willing to go just about anywhere to earn money for a better life. But the Italians were not English-speaking, and the Canadian government was trying to limit immigration from southern Europe. Bringing Italians to Canada was not going to be easy.

That's when two brothers, Vincenzo and Giovanni Veltri, stepped forward. They had first come to Canada in 1885, to work on the railway. As the demand for Italian labour began to grow, however, they saw a business opportunity. They set themselves up as labour agents, or *padroni*, and worked to bring their countrymen to Canada. Soon, other Italian Canadians were following their lead. The *padroni* made money taking fees from the employers, the steamship companies, and even the workers themselves. In return, the employers got employees, the steamship companies sold more tickets, and the workers were guaranteed passage to Canada and a job when they arrived.

Next to the Chinese, the Italians played the biggest role in pushing the Canadian Pacific Railway through the diamond-hard mountain rock and steep-sided river valleys of western Canada.

Not What They Bargained For

And thousands of young Italian men did begin to arrive. All found the jobs they'd been promised, but for many, Canada was not what they'd been expecting. Some *padroni* were dishonest, and they sent men to jobs that were dangerous and sites that were unsafe. Many Italians were shocked by the low wages being offered and the conditions they were made to live in. Often, they were housed in remote campsites that were freezing in the winter and plagued by blackflies in the summer. Money for food and rent was deducted directly from the men's paycheques—sometimes at five times the going rate. And if they got sick or were injured, they were simply out of work.

Of course, not all *padroni* were cheats, but enough of them were that they all got a bad name. In 1902, the Italian government even recommended restricting immigration to Canada until the abuses of the system were stopped. But most of the Italians who were already here decided it was better to put up with what they found than to return home empty-handed. They wanted to work, by hook or by crook. And work they did! From the mines and railways of British Columbia to the farms of Manitoba to the steel mills of Nova Scotia, they helped build the economy of their new home.

By the early 1900s, Italian men were bringing over their wives and children and making Canada their permanent home. In cities all over the country, Italian neighbourhoods known as "Little Italys" began to emerge.

Enemy Aliens

Over time, more Italians came to Canada. Between 1901 and 1910, about 60,000 of them made the long voyage overseas. Canadian cities were just then beginning to expand, and that attracted people with a whole new set of skills—bricklayers, stonemasons, shoemakers, and shopkeepers. Soon, whole sections of cities became Italian business districts, called "Little Italys."

But many Canadians continued to dislike Italian immigrants, and when Italy sided with Germany during the Second World War, their hostility grew. Italian shops were vandalized. And in some places, like the coal mines of Cape Breton Island, native-born Canadians refused to toil alongside their Italian-born co-workers.

The war eventually ended, however, and in its wake, immigration laws were relaxed. Thousands of immigrants from all over war-torn Europe flooded into Canada, and in 1947 Italians were taken off the list of so-called enemy aliens. Over the next fifteen years, more than 315,000 Italians came. Most of them settled in Canada's cities, where they opened small businesses like restaurants, tailor shops, barbershops, masonry firms, and grocery stores.

Today there are more than 1.3 million proud Canadians who claim Italian ancestry. In the last census, Italian was the fourth most common language spoken by Canadians, after English, French, and Chinese. There are Italian-Canadian newspapers, radio stations, television programs, and magazines. And Italians have also brought their love of food, fashion, art, and literature to Canada, enriching our culture in countless ways. In the end, it seems, their will to survive has been transformed into a passion to succeed.

Many early Italian immigrants were great entrepreneurs. They brought their skills with them from the Old World and bravely started new businesses in Canada.

During the Second World War, Italian Canadians were classified as "enemy aliens," and hundreds were sent to remote internment camps like this one in Kananaskis, Alberta.

A City of Neighbourhoods

Toronto is one of the most multicultural cities in the world. A walk through its busy downtown neighbourhoods offers the sights, sounds, and scents of India, Korea, Italy, China, Portugal, and Greece, among many other countries. It's like having the whole world magically reinvented on a bustling Canadian street!

This photo was taken at one of Toronto's six Chinatowns. The neighbourhood shops sell barbecued pork, steamed buns, duck, and bok choy. The many restaurants offer authentic Mandarin, Hunan, Szechuan, and Cantonese cuisine—with out-of-this-country flavours!

Waves of Greek immigrants came to Toronto after the Second World War. Many settled along Danforth Avenue, in the east end of the city. Stroll the street in summer and you'll see blue-and-white Greek flags hanging from windows, smell the moussaka and souvlaki cooking in restaurant kitchens, and hear Greek folk music being played on outdoor patios.

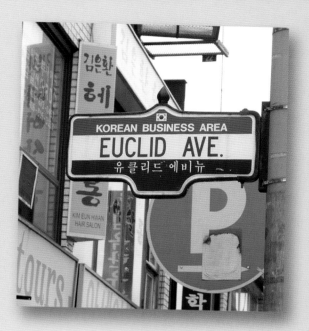

When an Indian woman wants to shop for a sari or a brightly coloured scarf, she heads for Little India, home to the Gerrard India Bazaar. Here, she can find traditional clothing, pick up some groceries, and then sip on some sugar-cane juice for a few minutes while she listens to the soundtrack of the latest Bollywood movie.

After the Canadian government introduced a more liberal immigration policy in 1967, a great number of Koreans moved to this country. Many now work and shop in Toronto's Korea Town. Here, travel agencies, bakeries, acupuncture clinics, gift shops, Internet cafés, and grocery stores cater to the Korean community—and everyone else as well!

This banner celebrates Little Italy, a downtown district that keeps its Italian flavour even though most Italians have actually moved farther north. The neighbourhood is alive with pool halls, trattorias, coffee shops, social clubs—and conversations that often include the word "soccer," a favourite Italian sport.

In the early 1960s, a local Portuguese restaurant became one of the meeting places for new Portuguese Canadians. "Everybody came there," remembers the owner. "People who were all alone in the city could meet each other there and talk and laugh and cry. They came to find friendship, and they did." Now Portugal Village is a bustling neighbourhood of bake shops, cheese shops, fish markets, and restaurants.

A New Century

The *Komagata Maru* Incident

During their two months of captivity, the passengers had to make do with the few supplies they already had aboard.

In 1908, the Canadian government passed a law that said all would-be immigrants had to come to Canada directly from their country of origin. Called a "continuous passage" order, this law disguised its real purpose, which was to bar immigrants from Asian countries like India and Japan. (There were no steamship lines providing service from those countries directly to Canada.) This pleased prejudiced white Canadians who disliked having Asians immigrate to their country.

A Sikh-Canadian businessman named Gurdit Singh was angry about the restrictive policy, however. He knew it would make it impossible for his fellow Sikhs from India to come to Canada, so in 1914 he decided to challenge the government. He thought that if he showed up with a boatload of Indian immigrants and contested the continuous-passage requirement, the government would give in and let his passengers stay.

So he chartered a Japanese steamer called the *Komagata Maru*. At the beginning of April, Singh set sail from Hong Kong for Vancouver with 376 passengers, the majority of them Sikh.

When the ship arrived after a month and a half at sea, only twenty-two of the passengers—all of them former residents of Canada—were allowed to disembark. The others were forced to remain aboard, anchored in the middle of Vancouver's harbour, until the government decided whether to let them stay.

Two long months passed. Throughout that time, the *Komagata Maru*'s passengers were basically kept prisoner. Officials didn't allow them to come ashore, and the ship wasn't even supplied with food or water.

Curious onlookers gathered on shore each day to stare out at the *Komagata Maru* and its captive passengers.

The Shore Committee

On land, meanwhile, the Shore Committee, a group of Indian Canadians and a handful of white supporters, began meeting and raising money to support the passengers. They sent telegrams to politicians in Canada and India, and eventually they mounted a legal challenge that went all the way to the Supreme Court of Canada.

In the end, the court ruled against the Sikhs, and Canadian immigration officials decided that the would-be immigrants would have to leave. At first, the ship's captain refused to go, arguing that he did not have enough food or water for the return voyage. But the Canadian navy was called in, and on July 23, 1914, the *Komagata Maru* was escorted out of the harbour by a navy cruiser. The Sikh community was devastated, their faith in the Canadian justice system shattered.

In recent years, India has been second only to China in the number of immigrants it provides to Canada. Not many of these immigrants come by boat any more, but most have heard the story of the *Komagata Maru*—the ship that challenged the government's discriminatory immigration policies. In May 1993, Canada at last issued a formal apology to its East Indian citizens for the *Komagata Maru* incident. It's a small gesture of remembrance for that boatload of expectant immigrants who would, in the end, be turned away.

All Aboard!

Until about forty years ago, almost all immigrants to Canada arrived by sea. All too often, ships were damp and dirty, and some weren't even seaworthy. In the early 1800s, the trip across the ocean could take as much as seven weeks. By the 1900s, it often took less than a week. But the journey usually wasn't over when the ship docked. Many immigrants still had hundreds—if not thousands—of kilometres to travel by train to reach their final destination.

This is a replica of a boat named the *Jeanie Johnston*, which brought Irish emigrants to Canada in the 1850s. All it took to turn this former cargo vessel into a passenger ship were some bunkbeds nailed along the walls in the steerage compartment. The overcrowded ship had no chairs or tables, and there was nowhere to escape the smell of seasick shipmates.

Passengers would do what they could to survive the long, monotonous days on the surging seas. In this 1910 photo, emigrants aboard the *Empress of Britain* gather on deck to jump rope—anything to make the voyage pass more quickly!

Steamship passengers made sure they filled in the information on their luggage tags and tied them with twine to their bags. Many also wore red identification tags of their own. When they got to port, they exchanged these for train tags that showed exactly where they were going.

This little Dutch boy has a train tag tied to his coat. The tag would have listed his ultimate destination, as well as the numbers of the train and the car he was supposed to travel in. Many immigrants could not speak English or French very well, so these tags served an important purpose. A train conductor could sneak a quick peek and help passengers find their proper seats.

Trains first began running in Canada in 1836. Just over fifty years later, passengers could travel the rails from coast to coast, as this map clearly shows. Chugging through the muskeg of northern Ontario, the vast expanses of the prairies, and the bold and mountainous terrain of the West, the Canadian Pacific Railway was the greatest engineering feat of its day.

The CPR designed special "colonist cars" for the new immigrants. At one end there was water and a stove for passengers to cook on; a washroom was at the other end. The cars had seats made of wooden slats that could be pulled out and turned into beds. An upper bed on hinges could be folded away when it wasn't in use.

The *Issei*

Top: These confiscated Japanese fishing boats give a sense of the extent of the wartime round-up. *Bottom*: In all, about 20,000 Japanese Canadians were interned, including this sad fisherman who has just lost his livelihood and his freedom.

Like the Sikh passengers of the *Komagata Maru*, the first Japanese to come to Canada were never welcomed into mainstream society. These early pioneers, known as the *issei*, were mainly peasant farmers and fishermen who left overcrowded Japanese villages and settled in British Columbia. Once here, they built temples and churches, and they opened schools and hospitals that operated in their own language. Slowly, they carved out a place for themselves and their Canadian-born children, called the *nisei*, in the New World.

But then life took a very cruel turn. On Sunday, September 10, 1939, Canada joined Britain's declaration of war on Germany. Eventually, this erupted into a global conflict, the Second World War, that pitted nations like Canada, the United States, and Great Britain against Germany and its allies, Japan and Italy. During the six years the war was waged, more than a million Canadian men and women travelled overseas to join the fight. Those who stayed behind grew scared. They began to question the loyalties of Canadians with German, Italian, or Japanese ancestry.

The Face of the Enemy

On December 7, 1941, Japanese planes bombed the American fleet in Pearl Harbor, Hawaii, and North Americans panicked. They saw, in their Japanese neighbours and friends, the face of the enemy. Suspicion consumed them. What if, Canadians wondered, the thousands of Japanese living along British Columbia's coast secretly supported the actions of their mother country? What if they were spies and planned to help Japan attack the West Coast by sea?

Fear pushed the government to act. Early in 1942, Mounties began rounding up all Japanese-Canadian males between the ages of eighteen and forty-five and moving them away from the coast of British Columbia. Children under eighteen, women, and adults over forty-five didn't fare much better. They had two weeks to get ready to relocate, and they had to leave behind everything except a few personal belongings. They would never get back any of the things they abandoned—houses, boats, cars, land. These things were sold, and they weren't even given the proceeds.

A father waves goodbye to his wife and daughter as they're taken off to a camp in the interior of British Columbia. Most of the men were separated from their families and sent away to labour camps.

At first, these prisoners of war were crowded into temporary facilities at city racetracks and exhibition grounds. Many were kept in large buildings that once had stabled livestock. Hundreds of makeshift bunkbeds lined the former stalls. There was no privacy, no peace and quiet. Some families spent days, weeks, or even months in these horrendous conditions before being sent on to more permanent camps.

The internees were expected to pay for their stay in the camps—even though they hadn't wanted to live there and almost everything they owned had been sold off without their permission.

When the day to relocate finally arrived, most families were separated. The men were sent to build roads or work on the railways. The women, children, and elderly were moved to internment camps far inland. (Many of these had been built by the first groups of Japanese men to be rounded up.) Life in these camps wasn't good. These Canadians weren't allowed any contact with the outside world. Their movements were restricted, and their mail was censored. People struggled to find a way to make this terrible situation tolerable.

Peace at Last

Years passed. Finally, on August 14, 1945, Japan surrendered. The war was over, but the struggle continued for the Japanese-Canadian internees. If they were lucky, they were moved from British Columbia to a former prisoner-of-war camp in Quebec, where they were assessed and eventually set free. The unlucky ones were stripped of their citizenship and deported to Japan by boat. And yet, not one Japanese Canadian was ever charged with spying.

When they were finally released, the remaining internees were not allowed to return to the homes and businesses they'd left behind.

Families had their freedom but almost nothing else. More than 4,000 Japanese Canadians opted to leave this nation.

Many of those who chose to stay lost their pride in their heritage. The *nisei* refused to teach their children, called the *sansei*, the Japanese language, and they stopped passing on traditional arts. The *sansei* grew up speaking English and knowing little of their ancestral homeland.

But time went by, and slowly attitudes began to change. Third- and fourth-generation Japanese Canadians began to learn their ancestors' language and to show interest in traditional Japanese culture. In 1977, Japanese communities across the country celebrated the hundredth anniversary of the arrival in Canada of the first Japanese. At the same time, they began to push harder for official recognition that they had been mistreated during the war.

Japanese Canadians have taken the dark thread that is their wartime sorrows and woven it together with the traditions of their ancestral home and the new traditions they discovered, and developed, in Canada. Through their perseverance and commitment to this nation, they have helped create the remarkable quilt that is Canada.

The three members of this proud family put on their best clothes as they prepared to be interned. In 1988, the government paid out about $12 million to compensate Japanese Canadians for the injuries done to them during the war.

Spotlight on
Life Must Go On

There was no freedom in the Japanese internment camps, but the people housed there refused to give up everything from their old lives. And so, they struggled to carry on. Children woke up early, had breakfast, and went to school. The few men who lived in the camps would head out to jobs in town or off to the fields to harvest berries. The women tended the sick at their community's hospital or manned the counter at the local store. Families gathered during spring and summer to watch the baseball teams practice and compete. These strong people were determined to do the best they could, whatever the circumstances.

The internees worked hard to turn their modest little houses into homes. Over time, rooms were added on, basements dug out, and bright curtains hung. On warm summer days, people ventured outside to tend their gardens and leave their laundry to flap in the breeze. If nothing else, the mountainous setting was among the most beautiful in the country.

Sometimes women had to make do with communal kitchens and woodstoves that were barely big enough for all their pots and kettles. All the buildings of the camps were made from simple wood siding with no insulation, and none had electricity or running water. In winter, internees would often have to sleep with all their clothes on just to keep warm.

Most communities had schools for grades 1 through 10. Enthusiastic young women with high school diplomas but no previous experience volunteered to try their hand at teaching. Many loved their new jobs so much that they were inspired to pursue teaching careers after the war.

Many camps had small stores where internees could buy canned goods and staples like rice and flour. Often, these became favourite gathering places. While they shopped, women could catch up with friends, plan community events, and simply enjoy getting out of the house with their children.

The internees kept their love of baseball alive. Some teams were so good that even the camp guards would wander over to watch them play. In time, players were allowed to travel from camp to camp for games, and they even ventured into nearby communities to take on local teams. Perhaps the common love of baseball helped to sweep aside some of the prejudice and fear that existed in the minds of many white Canadians.

Wartime Pioneers

The war brides represented the largest wave of immigration to Canada since well before the Second World War began.

Olive Madge Cochrane was a war bride. In 1942, the Londoner met a Canadian serviceman, Chamberlain "Lloyd" Cochrane, at a dance that her older brother had persuaded her to attend. Lloyd was smitten as soon as he saw Olive, and he spent most of the evening gathering up his courage to speak to her. When the dance was over, he walked her home, talking all the while. Just six weeks later, he proposed. Friends of Olive's saved up ration coupons so they would have enough eggs to make the couple a wedding cake.

Olive was just one of about 48,000 war brides, women who married Canadian servicemen who'd gone to Europe to fight during the Second World War. Most war brides came from England, Scotland, or

Wales, but others were from France, Belgium, Holland, and Italy. In all, about one in ten Canadian soldiers married while they were overseas.

When the war ended, however, the servicemen had to leave behind their new brides and return home with their fellow troops. It must have been difficult saying goodbye—most couples did not know when they would see each other again. But soon a move was afoot to reunite them. The Canadian government began making arrangements to move the thousands of women across the ocean to Canada, where they would join their husbands. In London, a Canadian Wives Bureau was set up to register the brides and assign them transportation.

Not all the brides came alone. In all, 22,000 children accompanied their mothers across the ocean. Many were excited to see their fathers, but some had been born while their dads were off fighting and had never even met them. And some were born aboard ship during the journey over!

Welcome to Canada

Olive and her son came to Canada in June 1946 on a massive ship called the *Queen Mary*. Like most war brides, Olive landed at Pier 21, the immigration station in Halifax. There, the women would disembark and be processed by immigration officers, and then they were free to go. Some were met at Pier 21 by their husbands, but many boarded trains for the next leg of their journey, often travelling thousands more kilometres through unfamiliar landscapes to reach their new homes.

Red Cross workers helped feed children whose mothers were too seasick to make it to their ship's dining room.

Many war brides had to travel great distances by train once they'd docked. A Canadian senator later said of them, "They were pioneers in the truest sense of the word."

Most war brides hadn't seen their husbands for a year or more, and many had never been away from home. They had no idea what to expect! Women from big cities like London and Glasgow must have been shocked when they stepped off the train in rural areas or remote small towns. For the first time, many were faced with the prospect of using outdoor toilets, drawing water from wells, and firing up wood-burning stoves for cooking and for warmth. In some cases, English-speaking war brides found themselves living in communities where everyone else spoke French. Their husbands sometimes had to struggle to find jobs, as postwar unemployment was high, and all the wives battled the loneliness that came from missing the friends and relatives they'd left behind. Special war brides clubs helped a bit. There, the women would talk about their homesickness, learn about life in this strange new land, and make plans for their future as Canadians.

In August 2000, the government erected a plaque in Halifax, Nova Scotia, to remember the war brides and what they gave to Canada. "Basically, we girls came out here, by and large not knowing what to expect," said one war bride. "The vast majority of us dug in, adapted, compromised, made homes for our husbands and families and became good contributing Canadian citizens." Another said simply, "I have never regretted coming to Canada and am proud to be a Canadian!"

When Olive docked in Halifax, she immediately sent Lloyd a telegram to let him know she'd arrived in Canada. But she still had a distance to go—all the way across the country to Vancouver!

GLOSSARY

ENGLISH	CANADIAN	ENGLISH	CANADIAN
Bank holiday	Legal holiday	Ladder	Run
Banknote	Bill	(in stocking)	
Basin	Mixing Bowl	Larder	Pantry
Beer or "Bitter"	Ale or beer	Lavatory	Toilet
Biscuit, sweet	Cookie	Lift	Elevator
unsweetened		Lounge suit	Business suit
Bill (in a	Check	Lorry	Truck
restaurant)		Luggage	Baggage
Block of Flats	Apartment house	Macintosh	Raincoat
Boiled Sweets	Candy (hard)	Made-to-order	Tailor made
Book a table	Reserve a place	Maize—	Corn
Book passage	Get Tickets	Indian corn	
Booking Office	Ticket Office	Motorcar	Automobile
Braces	Suspenders	Multiple stores	Chain Stores
Bureau	Writing desk or	Napkins (baby's)	Diapers
	Secretary	Paraffin	Coal oil
Cab rank	Taxi stand	Pavement	Sidewalk
Caretaker	Janitor	Petrol	Gasoline
Chemist	Druggist	Plate	Silverware
Chemist's shop	Drug Store	Plum cake	Fruit cake
Chest of drawers	Bureau	Pillar box	Mail box
(low)		Post (of a letter)	Mail
Cinema	Movies	Potato crisps	Potato chips
Corn	Grain	Pram	Baby carriage
Cotton wool	Absorbent cotton	Pullover	Sweater
Corset	Girdle	Reel of cotton	Spool of thread
Court shoes	Pumps	Return	Round trip
Cupboard	Closet	Rubber	Eraser
Curtains	Drapes	Scent	Perfume
Dickey	Rumble seat	Shooting	Hunting
Draper's shop	Dry Goods Store	Shopwalker	Floorwalker
Dress circle	Balcony	Silencer	Muffler
Dressing table	Dresser	(motor car)	
Dustbin	Garbage can	Single (ticket)	One way
Dustman	Garbage man	Sledge	Sled
Face flannel	Wash rag,	Spanner	Wrench
	wash cloth	Spirits	Liquor
First floor	Second floor	Stalls	Orchestra seats
Fishmonger	Fish dealer	Steadings	Farm buildings
Flat	Apartment	Stores	Groceries
	(or Flat)	(household)	
Frying pan	Skillet, frying pan	Suspenders	Garters
	or spider	Sweets	Candy
Galoshes	Rubbers	Sweet or savoury	Dessert
Gangway	Aisle	Tart	Pie
(theatre)		Teats	Nipples
Geyser	Water heater	Threepenny and	Five and Ten Store
Goods van, truck	Freight car	Sixpenny Bazaar	
Gramophone	Phonograph	Tinned	Canned
Greengrocery	Grocery store	Torch	Flashlight
Grilled	Broiled	Tram, tramway	Streetcar
Ground floor	First floor	Treacle	Molasses or syrup
Guard	Conductor or	Trunk call	Long distance
	brakeman	Tube	Subway
Haberdashery	Men's Wear	Undercut	Tenderloin
High boots	Boots	(of beef)	
High Street	Main Street	Upper circle	Second balcony
Hire purchase	Instalment plan	Valve (wireless)	Tube
Hoarding	Bill Board	Waistcoat	Vest
Ices	Ice Cream	Washing	Laundry
Ironmongery	Hardware Store	Wellingtons	Rubber boots
Joint	Roast	Wireless	Radio
Jug	Pitcher	Van	Truck
		Vest	Undershirt

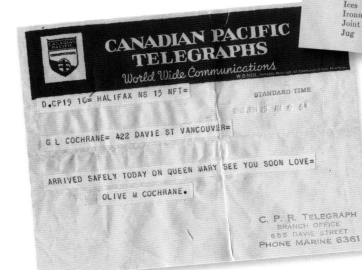

CANADIAN PACIFIC TELEGRAPHS
World Wide Communications

D.CP19 10= HALIFAX NS 15 NFT=

STANDARD TIME

G L COCHRANE= 422 DAVIE ST VANCOUVER=

ARRIVED SAFELY TODAY ON QUEEN MARY SEE YOU SOON LOVE=

OLIVE M COCHRANE.

C. P. R. TELEGRAPH
BRANCH OFFICE
655 DAVIE STREET
PHONE MARINE 6361

This glossary comes from a Department of National Defence booklet called "Welcome to War Brides." It explains the meaning of many words the war brides probably had never encountered before, including "apartment," "eraser," and "subway."

Spotlight on
The Gateway to Canada

After spending days crossing the ocean and waiting hours for their names to be called, some young immigrants had a hard time keeping their heads up and their eyes open.

For centuries, immigrants came to Canada by sea across the Atlantic Ocean. In the last century, most docked at Halifax, and from 1928 to 1971, more than a million passed through the doors of Pier 21, the immigration station that became the so-called Gateway to Canada.

Each day, ships docked with hundreds of passengers. Now began that nail-biting process that all new immigrants to Canada would share, no matter their country of origin or their dreams for the future. One after another, they would be processed through Pier 21. They would learn, finally, if they could stay in Canada.

At times, as many as 4,000 people needed processing, and that meant a lot of waiting and moving from room to room. Hundreds of weary, excited, anxious travellers sat on long wooden benches, bouncing babies on their knees and clutching passports in their fists. Others stood while waiting for their names to be called, arms crossed or hands jammed in pockets, too nervous to sit.

When they recognized their names, the new arrivals breathed a sigh of relief and headed off to the next room, families and belongings in tow.

Volunteer interpreters who spoke less common languages would respond promptly to a phone call from Pier 21 asking for help. Every new arrival was eventually paired up with someone who could help him or her understand the questions about to be asked.

Here there were wooden tables staffed by immigration officers who gave quick smiles and invited them to sit. Documents and immigration papers, carried possessively across thousands of kilometres, were handed over. The officers read quickly and carefully, going through the information with the tired travellers. "This is your name? This is where you were born? Where are you headed in Canada? Is all this correct?"

Many immigrants spoke no English or French, so the staff included interpreters who knew the most common languages—German, Italian, Dutch, and Russian. Once all newcomers were able to understand—and make themselves understood—there came the medical examinations, then luggage was inspected and sorted. The whole process took hours. But what were a few more hours after the days spent crossing the ocean and the weeks or months spent preparing for the long trip in the first place? And when the words "Landed Immigrant" were stamped on a new Canadian's immigration ID card, the long wait, the exhaustion, and the stomach-churning anxiety all melted away. Here was a fresh start. Here was a welcoming Canada.

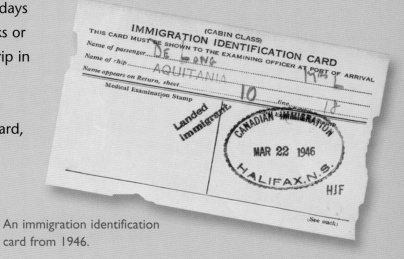

An immigration identification card from 1946.

81

The Displaced

By the time the Second World War ended, millions of Europeans had been scattered far from their homes. Citizens had fled countries in central, southern, and eastern Europe to avoid invading armies and escape terrible economic and political conditions. But the end of the war did not bring much improvement. Many refugees could not—or would not—return home. Some refused to go back to countries that had fallen under Communist rule. Others feared that the destruction brought by the war had left them without work, homes, family, or friends. Still others were Holocaust survivors who had no homes and no living relatives to return to.

Desperate, these so-called displaced persons gathered the little they had and migrated to special camps in Germany, France, Italy, and Belgium. Often, these were former labour or concentration camps—horrendous, inhuman places where barbed wire still ringed the high stone walls. People passed the time in these crowded, dirty conditions as best they could, but despair set in quickly when a temporary stay turned into a semi-permanent wait for resettlement. Some refugees would spend years in this limbo, waiting for their lives to begin again.

Eight-year-old Ausma Levalds was the 50,000th displaced person to come to Canada. She and her family left their native Latvia after the Soviet Union took it over. They spent more than three years in a camp in Germany before they were allowed to resettle in Ontario.

About 4,000 former Polish soldiers were among the first post-war refugees to arrive. They'd agreed to do a period of farm labour in return for the chance to emigrate. These men are about to board the train that will take them west to their new homes.

A Safe Haven

Canada, which had a great need for unskilled labourers, began extending a hand to those who had already suffered so much. But the Canadian government wasn't quite ready to open the door to just any newcomers. People from Britain, France, and northwestern Europe—immigrants who would most easily blend in—were at the top of Canada's "preferred" list, as were those who could provide labour in areas that were lacking. For many years, refugees could come to Canada only if they signed a contract promising to work for a period of time in farming, mining, the domestic service, or on the railway.

Most displaced persons, however, were so desperate to leave the camps behind that they gratefully accepted any type of work offered. In the years immediately following the war, 165,000 refugees found safe haven in Canada. Their years of suffering during the war would never be forgotten, but new experiences and fresh hopes lay ahead for the displaced people of Europe.

Young women like this one were at the top of Canada's "preferred" list. A domestic servant, she's happily helping to keep the farmhouse going while the men are out bringing in the harvest.

Spotlight on

A Home Away from Home

At times, Canada has been the temporary—and even permanent—host to large groups of desperate children from countries around the world.

Many children—more than 100,000 of them—came to Canada between 1869 and 1939 from childcare organizations in England, Wales, Scotland, and Ireland. Most of them were really too young to be on their own, as this 1894 ship's manifest shows. The doctor who signed this document declared that none of the children had inherited "any Disease or Deformity likely to make them unhealthy, or unsuited for Colonial life." After docking, they would have been sent out to work as domestics in Canadian homes or as labourers on farms.

These young immigrants were known as home children because they came from homes for the orphaned or destitute (poor). Some had mothers and fathers, however, but were sent away anyway—often without their parents' permission—because officials believed they would be better off in a land of fresh air and rolling green fields.

84

LEAVE THIS TO US SONNY — **YOU** OUGHT TO BE OUT OF LONDON

MINISTRY OF HEALTH EVACUATION SCHEME

This poster appeared on streets throughout Britain's major cities during the Second World War. Its message—"Get your children out of the city!"—was aimed at parents. The idea was to encourage Britons to move their children to places where they'd be safe from bombing campaigns and a potential German invasion, including friendly countries such as Canada and Australia. In the end, about 7,700 British children crossed the Atlantic Ocean during the Second World War to live with host families all across Canada.

Celina Lieber was just fourteen when she was given this identification card. As a Jewish Holocaust survivor with no home or family to return to, she was what was known as a displaced person. Celina's homeland, Poland, had been devastated by the war, and when she was given the opportunity to emigrate, she chose to go to Canada, a place she thought of as all "wilderness and the Arctic." She was joined by 1,122 other young Jewish orphans from fifteen different European countries as part of the War Orphans Project. The Canadian government agreed to let them come because the Jewish community had promised to support them. The needy children, most of them teenagers, found homes and a fresh start in thirty-nine communities across the country.

The Changing Face of Canada

An Education in a Suitcase

Although it lasted just eleven days, the Hungarian Revolution—a spontaneous uprising of ordinary citizens—changed the course of history.

The turmoil that followed the end of the Second World War eventually split the world into two main "blocs" of power. The Western bloc included countries like Canada and England and was led by the United States. The Eastern bloc was led by what was then the Soviet Union and included most of the nations of Eastern Europe. In the Eastern bloc, countries like East Germany, Poland, and Hungary came under strict Soviet control. But these had all once been free and independent nations, and opposition to the often repressive Soviet-backed regimes was high.

In Hungary, that opposition erupted into a spontaneous uprising in 1956. Ordinary Hungarians, many armed only with kitchen utensils

Many Hungarian refugees, like these, first came to Canada after the collapse of the Austro-Hungarian Empire at the end of the First World War. Others soon followed—to escape the Second World War and its aftermath, and then in the wake of the revolution. Today there are about 250,000 Canadians of Hungarian descent.

and other makeshift weapons, joined massive demonstrations designed to expel all Soviet troops from the country. The Soviets responded by sending in tanks to crush the rebellion.

Roughly 2,500 Hungarians lost their lives in the uprising, and another 250,000 fled the country between late 1956 and early 1957. Canada admitted about 37,000 Hungarian refugees, including hundreds of students and faculty members from the Forest Engineering University in the Hungarian city of Sopron. Tony Kuzak was one of those students. "It happened on November 4, 1956," he remembers. "We tried to defend Sopron from the approaching Soviet tanks, but we failed. Many of the students and professors left to avoid the cruelties expected from the Russians. We fled to Austria, [and] most of us did not take anything with us. I didn't even have an overcoat."

Class Is in Session

The dean of the university was among those who fled, and he soon realized that more than 300 students and about two dozen faculty members had also escaped. He and a few other professors decided to see if there was some way they could all continue their studies as a group. With the help of the Austrian government, he collected all the students and teachers together in one refugee camp, and then he began writing to foreign governments, looking for a new home. "Canada's response was the most generous," Kuzak explains. The government "agreed to adopt the staff and students of our two-hundred-year-old university [and fold it] into the University of British Columbia as a special faculty of forestry. The opportunities in British Columbia for foresters seemed the best in the whole world."

In January 1957, the students and faculty members came to Canada, their transportation paid for by the immigration ministry. The students and teachers spent the next several months learning English.

Time magazine named this anonymous revolutionary its man of the year for 1956. The Hungarian Revolution may have failed, but the fight for freedom and human rights lived on.

In Budapest, Canadian embassy officials rented out a dance hall so they would be able to process would-be refugees quickly and get them on their way to Canada.

Students came out in the hundreds to greet their counterparts from Hungary's Forest Engineering University at the Montreal train station in 1957.

Then, in September, their classes began again. The first year, all courses but one were offered in Hungarian. With each following year, one more course was taught in English.

Every year, students graduated. When the final group finished in the spring of 1961, a total of 141 Sopron students had completed the program. The graduates spread across Canada, most of them successfully finding work in the forestry sector. Today, almost a hundred are still practicing their profession in British Columbia.

"With the Hungarian Revolution still fresh in our memories," Kuzak says, "we felt responsible for the honour of Hungary. Because of this, despite language, social, and emotional difficulties, we carried on with our lectures and studying." He was rewarded for all his hard work with a teaching position of his own at UBC, and he soon settled down to start a family. Today he says, "It is obvious to me that Canada is the greatest country in the whole world."

Fasten Your Seatbelts

Not all immigrants made their way to Canada by boat and train. People used almost any mode they could think of—open rafts, rickety wagons, and eventually airplanes—to get to where they wanted to go. In 1964, for the first time, more than half of all newcomers arrived by air. Ever since then, more immigrants, refugees, and displaced persons have come to Canada by air than by sea.

Some immigrants settled in towns and cities, but many headed farther afield—to a homestead or someone else's farm, or to work in a mine or perhaps for a lumber company. Depending on where they were headed, they might have been directed towards the nearest river to hitch a ride aboard a small boat or raft. Others simply set out on foot or loaded their belongings into horse-drawn wagons borrowed from friends or hired from a local entrepreneur. Sometimes people had to use all these means of transportation, as this 1872 poster shows, to reach their final destination!

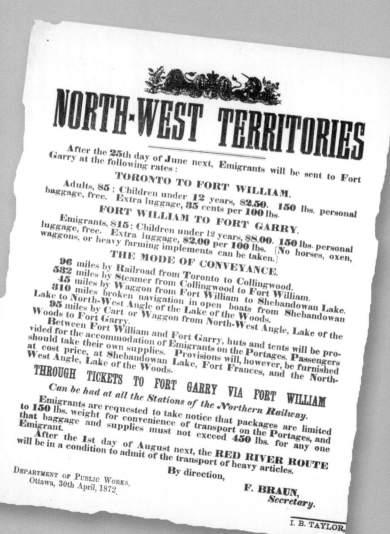

When American settlers were lured north in the 1890s, many travelled by train. But others couldn't afford the high ticket prices, so they journeyed to western Canada on "prairie schooners," or covered wagons, like these ones. The wagons were pulled by a team of horses or oxen and covered with a tarp to protect the settlers' meagre belongings.

By the early 1960s, airplanes were a common sight in the sky above Canada. They were also becoming a more popular way for immigrants to get to this country. Airline travel wasn't too expensive, and there were airports by then in many different countries.

On early flights, passengers were given cotton batting to protect their ears against noise and a cup in case this unfamiliar form of transportation proved too much for nervous stomachs. Hardly the lap of luxury—but airplanes did cut travel times from several days to several hours.

The Draft Dodgers

March on Washington November 15. End the War. Get Out Now!

Stop the war!
Stop the war machine!
Stop the death machine!

November 13-15
March Against Death: A Vietnam Memorial.
Delegations from every state representing
American war dead and Vietnam
villages destroyed, walking in a 36 hour
single file procession from
Arlington National Cemetery to the Capitol.

November 15
Assemble: 9:00am, Mall area
just west of 3rd Street NW
March: begins at 11:30am
Rally and Concert: Continuous Rally
and Folk Rock Concert 1-5pm
The Ellipse

November 16
continuing actions sponsored by
constituency groups.

I n the 1950s, the tension between the Eastern bloc and the Western bloc evolved into what came to be called the Cold War. This was not an actual conflict but a period of distrust and suspicion. Each side worried that the other was trying to spread its political system— democracy in the West and Communism in the East—throughout the world.

This is what the Americans thought was happening in Vietnam. In the mid-1950s, the country had been divided in two. When a guerrilla group from Communist North Vietnam began fighting against the American-backed South Vietnamese government, the United States decided to supply military and economic aid. The Americans feared that if South Vietnam fell to the Communists, other Asian nations would soon follow, like "a row of dominoes." Quite quickly, however, their support sucked them into a full-fledged war. By 1965, they had nearly 60,000 troops in the country.

The anti-war movement in the United States deeply divided the nation. To this day, Americans will still argue passionately for and against the Vietnam War.

Students burned their draft cards in a symbolic gesture that said, "We will not fight." Those who came to Canada entered the country as landed immigrants and did not have to reveal whether they were evading the draft.

The Tide Turns

At first, many Americans volunteered to fight in Vietnam. But as more and more troops were needed, voluntary enlistment wasn't enough. Soon, young people began to be drafted. At the same time, public opinion started to turn against the war. Thousands of U.S. soldiers were dying in a conflict that many Americans felt had nothing to do with them. With news reports bringing the reality of war into millions of homes every night, opposition grew. Large anti-war demonstrations took place on university campuses and in big cities across America.

Many draftees did not wish to fight. Those who refused faced jail time if they remained in the United States, however, so thousands decided to "dodge" the draft and head north to Canada. Canada was close by, uninvolved in the war, and didn't have any legal obligation to return draft dodgers to the U.S.

Between 1964 and 1977, somewhere between 50,000 and 125,000 Americans slipped across the border, most of them probably intending to stay only temporarily. But they found a nation whose citizens were, for the most part, more moderate and sympathetic than many of their own compatriots. When they had a chance to be pardoned in 1974, few were willing to agree. Some, still fearing prosecution and jail, dared not go back. Others chose not to. They had turned into Canadians.

In Foreign Territory

John Hagan was a draft dodger who left his home in Illinois for Edmonton in 1969. "Being born in a country is a different experience than becoming part of one," he explains. "Our new Canadian surroundings were a welcome alternative to military service in war-torn Vietnamese villages and jungles. Nevertheless, we were in foreign territory."

Coming to Canada was a tough decision for Hagan. "I will always remember my father warning in a departing phone call that this was the worst mistake I could ever make," he says. But Hagan never regretted it—and clearly most other draft dodgers didn't either. About three-quarters of the Americans who found refuge in Canada never returned to live in the United States again.

A Friend in Need

Americans who chose not to fight were not the only ones turning to Canada as a safe haven from the war in Vietnam. Thousands of Vietnamese refugees, like Timothy Tran of Toronto, came to this country in the war's aftermath. "When Communist North Vietnam invaded South Vietnam," Tran explains, "the whole country became Communist. Freedom [was] taken away from us. Human rights vanished. People lived in fear. No one could trust anyone. Many tens of thousands of South Vietnamese fled by boat in search of freedom and a new life."

These desperate escapees became known as boat people. They spent days at sea in perilous conditions, braving towering waves in unseaworthy boats. Many drowned or were attacked by pirates. But most landed on the shores of nearby countries, such as Malaysia, Thailand, and the Philippines, or were picked up by passing ships and dropped off at the ports of Singapore or Hong Kong. There they waited, hoping to be chosen for resettlement in a friendly country.

"I fled with my four brothers and one sister by boat in 1979," Tran recalls. (His parents had died in Vietnam.) "I was fifteen. We spent four days and three nights on the South China Sea, then arrived hungry and penniless in Malaysia. The United Nations High Commissioner for Refugees granted us status as political refugees, interviewed my family, and agreed to resettle us in Canada."

As many as one million refugees fled Vietnam, and the neighbouring countries of Laos and Cambodia, in tiny, rickety boats. Many then languished for years in overcrowded refugee camps.

Timothy Tran and his younger brother are seen here in Vietnam before the country was taken over. They made it to Canada, but their parents did not.

About 65,000 other Southeast Asians came to Canada as political refugees the same year as Tran. Many individual Canadians opened their homes and their hearts to these newcomers. They were taught English, helped to find jobs and homes, and given a hand adapting to the unfamiliar Canadian culture.

"We arrived with just a pair of shoes and the clothes on our body—no luggage," remembers Tran. "Our first task was to learn the new language. Then we started to work and save money for our future. My two older brothers and my sister were given jobs in a factory. My younger brother and I were sent to school. Life was difficult in the beginning. But we all worked and studied very hard."

In 1999, Tran was a clinical pharmacist working at a large Toronto hospital when he saw news footage of refugees being airlifted out of Kosovo, a war-torn province in what was once Yugoslavia. Five thousand of these refugees were on their way to Canada with only the clothes on their backs. When Tran learned this, he, like countless other Vietnamese Canadians, was eager to help. "I felt for these refugees fleeing the war," he says simply, "for I was once the victim of a similar situation."

Tran rushed to the air force base where the Kosovars were being housed and helped dispense medicine. "I felt proud to be a Canadian performing his duties and helping out the less fortunate," he remarks. "I felt strongly about giving something back to this great country of ours called Canada, for it has given me what I needed most: a new life."

More than 5,000 Kosovars were airlifted to Canada from refugee camps in Macedonia and Albania.

On the Edge

Like Vietnam, Afghanistan is a country with a tumultuous history. Tribes there have warred against one another for centuries, and neighbouring nations have invaded time and again. After two bloody internal revolts, the Soviet Union took over the vulnerable country in 1979. But conflict between those competing for power—the Soviets and their Afghan allies

As many as 2 million Afghanis still remain in refugee camps just outside their country's borders, too afraid to return.

against opposition groups funded by the United States, Pakistan, and Saudi Arabia—resulted in more violence. In just one decade, as many as one million people were killed.

After the Soviets pulled out in 1989, years of civil war followed. Then, in 1994, the Taliban, a radical Islamist political group, began to take over the country. The Taliban regime engaged in large-scale human-rights violations, and most nations refused to recognize it as a legitimate government. In 2000, the United Nations imposed trade sanctions against the country.

Vanished

Since the Soviets invaded in 1979, more than half of Afghanistan's 16 million citizens have vanished. Where have they all gone? Thousands were killed or injured in uprisings or in the civil wars that followed the Soviet withdrawal, but many simply fled their own country. In 1982, there were 3.2 million Afghani refugees in Pakistan alone. Many resolved not to linger in the misery and poverty of the refugee camps, waiting for peace in their own country. Instead, they struggled to make their way to distant Canada, where they have recreated some of the feel of their homeland in neighbourhoods known as "Little Kabuls." Ethnic restaurants and shops dot the streets, and in the local parks children fly colourful kites, an activity that was illegal under the Taliban regime. It's a second chance for everyone.

This little boy flies a kite given to him by Canadian soldiers, and enjoys the freedom he was denied by the Taliban.

Recently, political conditions in Afghanistan have changed again—this time, perhaps, for the better. The Taliban is gone, and a temporary government is in place. Many countries, including Canada, have re-established diplomatic relations with Afghanistan. Displaced Afghanis are now faced, again, with a tough decision: Should they go back home? Many want to help rebuild their country, but others have put down roots and aren't willing to give up what they've created in Canada. They're not certain that Afghanistan really is "home" any more.

In the meantime, they're doing what they can to help from here. Organizations have sprung up across the country as concerned citizens search for ways to raise funds and collect items that the people of Afghanistan desperately need. And the tragedy that brought Afghanis to Canada has also taken Canadians to Afghanistan. For several years, Canadian soldiers have been in the country helping to provide military support, build schools, drill wells, and deliver aid to all those who need it.

All over Afghanistan, the work of rebuilding the country is under way.

Spotlight on

Read All about It

For almost a century, new arrivals to Canada have been writing and publishing newspapers in their native tongues. The ethnic press has filled many roles for new citizens, introducing them to unfamiliar laws and customs, guiding them to jobs and places to live, and easing the transition from one culture to another. Today, millions of Canadians from coast to coast to coast are served by papers in languages other than English and French.

For more than fifty years, the *Corriere Canadese*, or "Canadian Courier," has brought news to Toronto's large and influential Italian community. It is the only Italian-language daily in the country. The newspaper also publishes an English-language weekly called *Tandem*, which targets second- and third-generation Italian Canadians.

The Chinese-language *Sing Tao Daily* is one of the most successful ethnic newspapers. It publishes seven days a week, 365 days a year, and offers separate editions for British Columbia, Alberta, and Eastern Canada. Its name in English means "Starry Island," perhaps a reference to the twinkling city lights of Hong Kong, where its sister paper was born more than sixty years ago.

The weekly *Indo-Canadian Times* has served Sikh Canadians since 1978. Written entirely in the Punjabi language, the Vancouver-based newspaper covers politics and current events in Canada, India, and around the world. It is the best-selling Punjabi newspaper in North America.

Turkish Canadians can pick up a copy of the Montreal-based *Bizim Anadolu* and leaf through it over a cup of piping hot Turkish coffee, one of their best-known imports to this country. The trilingual (Turkish, English, and French) newspaper began publishing in 1994. Its name means "Our Anatolia" and refers to the large peninsula that is the heart of Turkey.

These papers serve the Ukrainian, Icelandic, and Portuguese communities. They are just three of the hundreds of ethnic and foreign-language newspapers that are published in Canada. Readers can get their news in virtually every language of the globe, including Urdu, Farsi, Latvian, Finnish, and even Gaelic, the nearly extinct ancient tongue of Ireland.

White Flakes Falling from the Sky

Millions of Somalis fled to refugee camps in neighbouring countries to escape the civil war and famines that have plagued their country. Some people have spent years in these camps, waiting for their lives to improve.

I f people come together," says a traditional Somali proverb, "they can even mend a crack in the sky." That's a wonderful metaphor for the Somali community in Canada. Since 1990, tens of thousands of Somalis have fled starvation and civil war in their North African homeland. Many of them ended up in Toronto, where there were already many Somali Canadians ready to help the new arrivals—showing them around, getting them schooling, and finding them jobs and places to live. Today those second-wave Somali immigrants have become teachers, police officers, and social workers, and they're now giving back to their community as well. To heal themselves after the great losses they suffered in Somalia, they have had to reach for the sky in Canada.

But imagine what it must have been like for these people when they first arrived. Most were unable to speak English, and they had come with only the faintest idea of what Canada was like. What a shock it must have been to set down in a place where absolutely everything—

Heavily armed Somali warlords have kept their country in turmoil for more than a decade.

the weather, the food, the landscape—was different. For people used to the burning sun of north-eastern Africa, that first sight of white snowflakes falling from the sky must have been almost magical.

Mixed Emotions

Although these new Canadians were certainly happy to be safe, their arrival here was probably bittersweet. In many cases, families couldn't afford to come all at the same time, and fathers often stayed behind in Somalia with one or more children. The newcomers had to get used to life without husbands and fathers, brothers and sisters. They had to get used to new schools, new jobs, new friends, and new neighbourhoods. They knew it could be many years before they felt truly at home in this land.

That's why it was a life-saver to have other Somali Canadians lend a hand. The sooner people were settled and established, the sooner they were able to send money back home to those struggling to get by. Today many Somali Canadians are trying to make a difference on a grander scale as well. Volunteer organizations are working hard to improve Somalia's prospects for the future, promoting sustainable development, healing victims of war, and fighting to bring poverty to an end. These people have seen that cracks in the sky can be mended. Together, they are helping others make the traditional Somali proverb come true.

Traditionally, women pound leaves with a mortar and pestle to make henna powder.

Mehndi

Women in Somalia use henna, a greenish-yellow powder made from a plant, to decorate their hands and legs for important events, such as weddings. This practice, called mehndi, has been around for thousands of years, and immigrants have recently brought it to Canada.

Today, imitation henna tattoos are popular with young Canadians. Anyone can buy them, wet them, and press them on, decorating their hands and legs with temporary designs. This is a piece of North African culture that has crossed the ocean and gripped the imagination of Canadians.

103

Spotlight on
The Changing Face of Canada

Every day, people from countries around the world make Canada their home. In recent years, Canadian immigrants have come primarily from these ten countries: China, India, Pakistan, the Philippines, South Korea, the United States, Iran, Romania, the United Kingdom, and Sri Lanka. Some new immigrants have been pushed from their own country by circumstances there, while others have been pulled towards Canada by what they hope to find here. How does it feel to begin again somewhere new? Listen to the stories of these recent arrivals.

"I was born in Korea and lived there until I was four years old. I also lived in Hong Kong for about eight years. We moved to Toronto in 2001. I was very happy about the new house I was going to live in. I felt excited about moving to a new country and having new friends. But at the same time, I felt sad about leaving Hong Kong and my old friends. I think Canada is a great place to live. Everybody is very nice and comforting. I love it when it's winter here, but sometimes it gets too cold."

—Jinoo Muther

"I came to Canada with my husband in 2000 from Guangzhou, in China. In general, we had a good living there. We had our own apartment, and no worries about how to make a living. But we wanted to live in a country with clean air, not much pollution, rich natural resources, no heavy traffic jams, big space. And we wanted a country that could give us more fairness, more equality. Because we cannot communicate in English as fluently as we can in Chinese, we cannot get the same jobs as we had in China. However, we accept this change. We now have a Canadian-born daughter who will get the benefit from the education system here, and we hope she will have a much better future than us."

—Rena Yang

104

"I'm originally from Iran. I came to Canada in 2001. I wanted to experience a new place, and to explore, see, and feel for myself the things that I had heard about. I'm a civil engineer. Unlike many immigrants, I was lucky enough to be able to find a job here and work in my profession. I live in Toronto, and Iranians have a big community here, so I don't miss Iran too much. I do my shopping in Iranian stores and even my barber is an Iranian! I really like that many different people from different origins and different beliefs, cultures, and religions live peacefully together. I still feel connected to Iran, but now I am an Iranian Canadian."

—Mohammed Aman

"I am originally from Romania. In March 1998, I came to Canada. Leaving home was a difficult experience. It was hard to say goodbye to a life I knew so well, even though there was an adventure waiting at the other end. But this experience has helped me understand more about myself, my real strengths. I would have never known my limits if I had not chosen to come."

—Manuela Stefan

"I am from India. I came to Canada in June 2003. I was very excited to see this country. I knew it had different people and a modern lifestyle that I could learn about only on television and from reading books. But I felt an emptiness as the day of moving came near. I was very sad to leave my dear grandparents and friends. I wondered, Will I feel out of place? Will I have any friends? It took me two or three months to get used to being here. My school friends and teachers helped me a lot. I feel Canada is a wonderful place. I am enjoying all the changes. But sometimes it is difficult too."

—Elattuvalappil Parvathy

"I was born in Sri Lanka. I am Tamil. I left my country because government forces were suppressing the Tamil people. Innocent people were being killed. Even though I love my country, I had to leave. I came to Canada in 1999. This is a beautiful country, and I have found freedom here. Canada supports human rights. It is the best country in the world."

—Ghanesh Sinnappu

TIMELINE

1497–98 Giovanni Caboto makes two voyages from Bristol, England, to fishing grounds near Newfoundland.	
1535 The name Canada is used for the first time.	**1608** Samuel de Champlain founds a permanent French colony at Quebec.
1620 English settlers come to Massachusetts aboard the ship the *Mayflower*.	**1663–65** France's King Louis XIV sends troops, an administrator, and settlers to New France.
1670 The Hudson's Bay Company is given fur-trading rights to all lands draining into Hudson Bay.	
1763 France gives up all its colonies in North America except St-Pierre and Miquelon and Louisiana.	**1755** British soldiers expel the Acadians from Nova Scotia.
1775–83 The Thirteen Colonies fight the American Revolution to gain their independence from Britain.	**1783–84** United Empire Loyalists make their way to Nova Scotia, Quebec, and what would become New Brunswick and Ontario.
1834 Slavery is outlawed throughout the British Empire. American slaves journey to freedom on the Underground Railroad.	
1845–50 The Great Potato Famine kills almost a million in Ireland.	**1847** Thousands of Irish immigrants cross the sea to Canada on rickety "coffin ships."

World Events		Canadian Immigration Events	
Ontario, Quebec, Nova Scotia, and New Brunswick come together to create the Dominion of Canada.	**1867**		
		1872	The government passes the Dominion Lands Act to try to attract immigrants to the prairies.
The Canadian Pacific Railway is built.	**1875–85**		
		1885	The Chinese Immigration Act is passed. A head tax on Chinese immigrants is set at $50.
Gold is discovered in the Klondike.	**1896**		
		1891–1914	Approximately 170,000 Ukrainian immigrants come to Canada.
		1906	Canada passes its first official Immigration Act.
		1910	The second Immigration Act is passed.
The Armistice, a peace agreement, is signed on November 11, bringing the First World War to an end.	**1918**	**1923**	The Chinese Exclusion Act is passed. With few exceptions, it prevents "any immigrant of any Asiatic race" from coming to Canada.
The stock market crash marks the beginning of the Great Depression.	**1929**		
		1931–41	Immigration plunges from more than a million in the previous ten years to only 140,000 people.
Britain and her allies declare war on Germany, Italy, and Japan.	**1939**	**1947**	Canada adopts the Canadian Citizenship Act. This act confers citizenship on both native-born and naturalized Canadians for the first time.

World Events	Canadian Immigration Events

Canadian Immigration Events

1952 The third Immigration Act is passed. It focuses mainly on who should be refused entry to Canada.

Thousands of citizens fill the streets of Budapest during the Hungarian Revolution. — **1956**

1956–57 More than 37,000 Hungarians are admitted to Canada.

1960 The Canadian Bill of Rights is introduced.

The Soviet Union invades Czechoslovakia. — **1968**

1968–69 More than 10,000 Czech refugees enter Canada.

1971–72 Canada receives more immigrants from the United States than from any other country.

The city of Saigon falls to the North Vietnamese, marking the end of the Vietnam War. — **1975**

1976 A new Immigration Act focuses on family reunification and the fulfilment of Canada's economic and cultural needs.

Soviet troops invade Afghanistan. — **1979**

1991-2001 Almost 2 million immigrants arrive in Canada.

Conflict erupts in the Kosovo region of southern Yugoslavia. — **1998**

2001 The Immigration and Refugee Protection Act places greater emphasis on a refugee's need for protection and less on the ability to resettle in Canada.

A tsunami claims thousands of lives in Indonesia, Thailand, and Sri Lanka. — **2004**

FURTHER RESOURCES

People from every country in the world now call Canada home. This book has introduced you to just some of them. If you want to learn more about the immigrants who have helped build this country or about your own family's background, here are some online resources that can help.

www.cbc.ca/news/becomingcanadian/index.html
Could you become a Canadian citizen? Find out by logging onto this CBC site.

www.genealogy.gc.ca
The website of the Canadian Genealogy Centre can help you begin to trace your family's roots. Click on Activities on the Genealogy at School page to follow the Odyssey of Our Ancestors or take the Migration Challenge!

www.cic.gc.ca
Explore this Citizenship and Immigration Canada site to find out more about the Canadian refugee system and our immigration laws.

citzine.ca
Check out this Citizenship and Immigration Canada online magazine for kids. It includes games and quizzes!

www.thememoryproject.com
The Dominion Institute's Memory Project has pages where famous authors tell of their own experiences coming to Canada. A digital archive uses written and audio interviews, photographs, and artifacts to tell stories of immigration to this country. You can even access an online database of interviews with ordinary Canadians or submit your own story!

www.histori.ca
The Historica Foundation website is chock full of information about Canadian history. Check out the one-minute videos to see the story of the Underground Railroad and events like the Halifax Explosion brought to life.

www.canadianhistory.ca/iv
Immigrant Voices offers an informative historical overview of immigration to Canada. The site includes images, maps, graphs, and documents.

www.collectionscanada.ca/05/0509_e.html
Click on Newcomers in the National Archives' Living Memory exhibit to look at historical documents, photos, and artifacts that illustrate Canada's diversity.

www.ourroots.ca
The Our Roots website gives you online access to Canada's local histories.

www.pier21.ca
Go to the Pier 21 Society website to learn more about all the people who passed through the Gateway to Canada between the 1920s and the 1970s.

www.diversitywatch.ryerson.ca/backgrounds
Ryerson University's Diversity Watch website provides fact sheets for many different ethnic groups within Canada.

www.whitepinepictures.com/seeds
The Scattering of Seeds: The Creation of Canada is the website for a television series celebrating the contributions made by immigrants to Canada. You can read about the episodes and watch video clips online.

Acknowledgements

I wish to thank Janice Weaver for her editorial work on this book and Anne Shone for locating so many of the gorgeous visuals that appear in it. I would also like to acknowledge the assistance of the following people: Mohammed Aman; Will Armstrong; Esther Bryan, the Invitation Project; Irvine Carvery, the Africville Genealogy Society; John Hagan; Melynda Jarratt; Marshall-Shibing Jiang; Yanwei (Vivian) Jiang; Les Jozsa; Tomas Kubinek; Prof. Tony Kuzak; Dr. David Lai; Khanh Le, the Vietnamese Association; Diane McCord, the United Empire Loyalists' Association of Canada, Toronto branch; Jinoo Muther; Paul Muther; Elattuvalappil Parvathy; Aly-Khan Rajani, CARE Canada; Michelle Rusk; Ghanesh Sinnappu; Manuela Stefan; Timothy Linh Tran; and Rena Yang.

Photo Credits

Care has been taken to trace ownership of copyright materials contained in this book. Information enabling the publisher to rectify any reference or credit line in future editions will be welcomed.

For reasons of space, the following abbreviations have been used:
BCA: British Columbia Archives
CMC: Canadian Museum of Civilization
CP: Canadian Press
CPRA: Canadian Pacific Railway Archives
CSTM: Canada Science and Technology Museum
CVA: City of Vancouver Archives
GA: Glenbow Archives
LAC: Library and Archives Canada
NGC: National Gallery of Canada
NSARM: Nova Scotia Archives and Records Management
PC: Parks Canada
PH: Picture History

Front cover and page 1: (background) LAC/C-014031; upper left (ration card): private collection; upper middle (identity card): Delia Matthews; upper right (family photo): LAC/C-046355; centre (coin): National Currency Collection, Currency Museum, Bank of Canada, Gord Carter; lower left (boy photo): LAC/PA-152023; lower middle (document): NSARM/MG 1 vol. 948 no. 196 (mfm. no. 14960); lower right (family photo): GA/NA-748-83; back cover: upper left (telegram): Michelle Rusk; upper right (photo): LAC/PA-147114; lower left (boy and girl photo): LAC/C-046355; lower right (background document): LAC/C-149236; lower right (foreground photo): CP/AP/Andrew England; page 3: GA/NA-3342-2; 4: LAC/C-065432; 5: LAC/C-004745; 6–7: Invitation: The Quilt of Belonging/photos Ken McLaren; 8: CMC/catalogue no. BgFp-32:20 and BgFp-32:244; 9: LAC/PA-116147; 10 (upper): BCA/I-21971; 10 (lower): CMC/catalogue no. DjMd-2:161/photo Jean-Luc Pilon/Manitoba Museum Collection; 11 (upper): CMC/catalogue no. KbFk-7:308/photo Merle Toole; 11 (lower): CMC/catalogue no. GbTo-18:297/photo Ross Taylor; 12: LAC/C-002706; 13: LAC/C-000168; 14: LAC/C-002706; 15: PC/F. Cattroll/H.03.30.01.20(16); 16: LAC/C-073709; 17 (upper): PC/T. Grant/H.03.36.04.04(02); 17 (lower): PC/A. Guindon/H.03.36.06.18(01); 18: LAC/C-073716; 19: LAC/C-020126; 20: LAC/POS-000267; 21: LAC/C-000168; 22 (upper): LAC/C-001512; 22 (lower): LAC/C-014031; 23: LAC/C-132561; 24: Kings Landing Historical Settlement, New Brunswick/photo courtesy of Faith Thomas; 25: LAC/C-002001; 26: National Archives, UK/CO5/1353; 27 (upper): LAC/C-0401621/W.H. Cloverdale Collection of Canadiana; 27 (lower): LAC/C-115424; 28: *The Underground Railroad*/Charles T. Webber/Cincinnati Art Museum, Subscription Fund Purchase; 29 (upper): GA/NA-748-83; 29 (lower): GA/NA-3556-1; 30: NSARM/MG 1 vol. 948 no. 196 (mfm. no. 14960); 31 (upper): NSARM/Bob Brooks fonds; 31 (lower): reprinted with permission from The Halifax Herald Limited; 32: NGC (no. 7157)/*Cholera Plague, Quebec c. 1832*/Joseph Légaré; 33: LAC/C-147016; 34: LAC/PA-136924; 35: LAC/PA-122657; 36: LAC/PA-046790; 37 (upper): PC/R. Seale/H.05.46.01.07(01); 37 (lower): PC/P. McCloskey/H.05.46.01.20(20); 38: LAC/C-003693; 39: CPRA/BR.195; 40: LAC/C-003693; 41: CPRA/A.6399; 42 (upper): GA/NA-3740-29; 42 (lower): LAC/C-149236; 43: LAC/C-072064; 44: GA/ND-2-109; 45 (upper): LAC/C-023415; 45 (lower): PC/J. Butterill/H.06.61.06.15(75); 46: Nelson Gerrard; 47 (upper): Nelson Gerrard; 47 (lower): *The Landing at Willow Point*/Arni Sigurdson/photo courtesy of the New Iceland Heritage Museum; 48: GA/NA-2438-3; 49: David Jón Fuller/Lögberg-Heimskringla; 50 (left): LAC/e002712081; 50 (right): LAC/C-063256; 51 (upper left): CPRA/A.6043.1; 51 (upper right): GA/P4346-A-10; 51 (lower left): LAC/e002712082; 51 (lower right): LAC/C-052819; 52: CPRA/BR.195; 53 (upper): LAC/C-004745; 53 (lower): LAC/C-005115; 54: GA/NA-3800-1; 55: NGC (no. 30836.6)/*The Ukrainian Pioneer, No. 6*/William Kurelek/with permission of the Isaacs Gallery; 56: LAC/C-024880; 57 (upper): GA/NA-1000-7; 57 (lower): LAC/C-005131; 58: GA/NA-4148-2; 59: GA/ND-9-36; 60: GA/NA-3342-2; 61 (upper): LAC/PA-123090; 61 (lower): GA/NA-5124-22; 62–63: Greg Hall; 64: CSTM/CN000443; 65: Pier 21; 66: CVA 7-123; 67: CVA 7-129; 68 (left): The Jeanie Johnston Company; 68 (right): LAC/C-009660; 69 (upper left): Vancouver Museum Collection/H990.277.5; 69 (upper right): Pier 21; 69 (lower left): LAC/NMC-11863; 69 (lower right): GA/NA-978-4; 70 (upper): LAC/PA-037467; 70 (lower): LAC/PA-134097; 71: LAC/C-057249; 72: LAC/C-046350; 73: LAC/C-046355; 74 (left): LAC/PA-142853; 74 (right): LAC/C-024452; 75 (upper): LAC/C-024454; 75 (middle): LAC/C-027623; 75 (lower): Pat Adachi/Ken Kutsukake; 76: LAC/PA-147114; 77 (upper): LAC/PA-175792; 77 (lower): Delia Matthews (with the assistance of www.WeddingsPastandPresent.co.uk); 78: CSTM/CN000443; 79 (upper): Pier 21; 79 (lower): Michelle Rusk (with the assistance of www.WeddingsPastandPresent.co.uk); 80: LAC/PA-152023; 81 (upper): LAC/PA-181009; 81 (lower): Pier 21; 82: Pier 21; 83 (upper): CSTM/CN000987; 83 (lower): LAC/C-137978; 84 (upper): LAC/C-147042; 84 (lower): LAC/PA-041785; 85 (upper): Imperial War Museum, London; 85 (lower): Vancouver Holocaust Education Centre © Celina Lieberman; 86: CP/Stephen Thorne; 87: CP/Andrew Vaughan; 88: CP/AP; 89: CSTM/CN000446; 90 (upper): Getty Images; 90 (lower): LAC/C-007108; 91: LAC/PA-147714; 92: LAC/NLC-004856; 93 (upper left): GA/NA-237-9; 93 (upper right): CPRA/A6671; 93 (lower): CPRA/M.4781/N. Morant; 94 (upper): PH/1970.0022; 94 (lower): PH/1960.0626; 95: PH/1960.0582; 96: CP/AP/Eddie Adams; 97 (upper): Timothy Tran; 97 (lower): CP/Andrew Vaughan; 98: CP/AP/Matiullah Achakzai; 99 (upper): CP/Stephen Thorne; 99 (lower): CP/AP/Manish Swarup; 100 (left): Corriere Canadese; 100 (right) Sing Tao Daily; 101 (upper left): Indo-Canadian Times International Inc.; 101 (upper right): Bizim Anadolu; 101 (lower left): Lögberg-Heimskringla; 101 (lower centre): Kobzar Publishing Co. Ltd.; 101 (lower right): Corriere Canadese; 102: CP/AP/Andrew England; 103 (upper): CP/AP/Sayyid Azim; 103 (lower): © The Cover Story/CORBIS; 104–105: NOAA/NGDC; 112: CP/Andrew Vaughan.